PARENTS, PREGNANT TEENS AND THE ADOPTION OPTION

Help for Families

By Jeanne Warren Lindsay

Morning
Glory
Press

Buena Park, California

Library of Congress Cataloging-in-Publication Data

Lindsay, Jeanne Warren.
   Parents, pregnant teens and the adoption option.

   Bibliography: p. 197-204.
   Includes index.
   1. Adoption–United States. 2. Teenage mothers–
United States–Attitudes. 3. Birthparents–United States–Attitudes.
4. Grandparents–United States–Attitudes. I. Title.
HV875.55.L553 1989   362.7'34'0973   88-8359
ISBN 0-930934-29-6. Cloth.
ISBN 0-930934-28-8. Paper.

MORNING GLORY PRESS, INC.
6595 San Haroldo Way   Buena Park, CA 90620
Telephone (714) 828-1998

Printed and bound in the United States of America

To the wonderfully caring
and courageous birthgrandparents
who share their experiences so freely
on these pages.

CONTENTS

PREFACE

Pregnancy counseling is available in many areas for pregnant teenagers and their partners. *Their* parents, however, may feel very alone as they realize their teenager needs their support now more than ever. Many parents provide that support and, after delivery, cherish the new grandchild as grandparents have always done.

Others, however, support their daughter (or son) as an adoption plan is made and carried out. For these parents, there is no joy in becoming grandparents because there is no baby to hold and to cherish.

They may feel strongly that adoption is the best plan given the circumstances, but losing their grandchild to another family is a painful process. This book is written directly to these mothers and fathers of birthparents.

Birthgrandparents – those who lose a grandchild through the process of adoption of that child by another family – are likely to have little or no support from anyone. They may not want to talk about their daughter's pregnancy.

Their friends may not know how to approach them for fear of offending them. Many birthgrandparents feel terribly alone during this time.

Birthgrandparents who share their stories here have felt that aloneness. They have grieved for the grandchild who will never be theirs. Over and over they talk about their need for counseling, for a support group. A few have started such a group, sharing their pain and their empathy with other hurting parents.

A book can never replace a support group. Spending time with people who have been through similar experiences can be extremely helpful for those who are dealing with crisis in their lives.

People, however, can get a lot of help from relevant books. Judy Glynn, Axtell, Kansas, looked for such a book several years ago when her 15-year-old daughter, Laurie, was pregnant. Laurie was given a copy of *Pregnant Too Soon: Adoption Is an Option,* and Judy read it with her. Judy wondered if there was a similar book written for parents.

"Our daughter needs help and support most of all, and we appreciate the help she's getting," Judy wrote, "but we need help, too. Do you know of a book for us and other parents in our situation?" This book is meant to provide that help.

In fact, Judy and Jim Glynn are an integral part of *Parents, Pregnant Teens and the Adoption Option*, this book finally written in response to Judy's letter. With the approval of their three children, Judy and Jim agreed to share the extensive journal they wrote during Laurie's pregnancy and for several months afterward. It is a wonderful description of their feelings as they faced their daughter's pregnancy, and a sensitive, caring and loving testimonial to the support they provided for Laurie when she needed them. The Glynn journal is reprinted beginning on page 155.

Experiences of many other birthgrandparents are included in this book. In fact, these birthgrandparents provide the written equivalent of a support group. They talk about their shock at learning their daughter is pregnant or their son has caused a pregnancy. They discuss the practical things they needed to do in dealing with too-early pregnancy.

And, as the title implies, this group of parents talks about considering an adoption plan for their grandchild. They discuss their daughter's/son's needs, and the absolute necessity of the birthmother and birthfather being able to make their own decision concerning releasing the baby for adoption or rearing the baby themselves. The people speaking through these pages are almost entirely parents of young people who did carry through with adoption plans for their babies.

They stress the support their daughter or son needed as s/he grieved for the loss of the baby after the adoption. These grand-parents also talk about their own grieving, and suggest ways of dealing with it. They talk about going on with their lives after experiencing too-early pregnancy and adoption within their families.

As the writer, I have stayed in the background just as I would if I were leading a support group in person for birthgrand-parents. Sharing others' experiences in a constructive, healing manner is a goal of a support group. This book has the same goal.

You will find very little here about the legal aspects of adoption because this is covered to some extent in *Pregnant Too Soon: Adoption Is an Option*. Adoption law, however, varies from state to state and from province to province. Anyone considering an adoption plan should be well informed on the law. An adoption agency counselor is a good source for this kind of information.

I'm often frustrated as I read the adoption literature at the strong emphasis still placed on the adoptive parent corner of the adoption triangle. Adoption is still considered by many people simply to be a way of supplying babies to childless families. Families from which those babies originally came are not given much consideration. The birthmother, the birthfather, and the entire birthfamily generally remain in the shadows even today.

Recently I received a long letter from a would-be adoptive grandmother in which she described in detail the heartbreak her entire family was experiencing over the "loss" of the baby her son and his wife had expected to adopt, a loss caused by a birthmother deciding to keep her child to rear herself.

I felt the pain of the adoptive family, yes, but I was chagrined to find that adoptive grandmother failed even to mention the pain the birthfamily would have faced had the adoption plan been carried out. *Someone always hurts in adoption.*

This book is meant to help birthgrandparents cope with their teenager's untimely pregnancy and with the pain of adoption, if that is the plan for the baby. It is also meant to offer insight to *adoptive* parents concerning the love and the caring their child experienced in his/her first family. Adoptees who know very little or nothing about their birthfamilies may also find comfort in these pages as they realize their birthfamilies, too, undoubtedly released them for adoption, not because they were "throwing them out," but because their birthparents loved them and wanted a better life for them than they could provide at that time.

Only a few birthparents share their experiences in this book because I chose not to repeat the contents or the purpose of *Pregnant Too Soon*. Birthparents, of course, make the adoption decision, and birthparents are even closer to their baby than are that baby's birthgrandparents. However, *Parents, Pregnant Teens and the Adoption Option* is written for the grandparents as they struggle to cope with too-early pregnancy in their families, and the tremendously difficult decision – to keep the baby in their family or release that child to another waiting family.

Over and over the voices on these pages tell us, "We're hurting, but we can handle it. We only want what's best for the baby and for our daughter (or son)."

This book truly is about love.

FOREWORD

In the past, stigma and secrecy were associated with an out-of-wedlock pregnancy. Today, of course, the stigma is largely gone, but the crisis of an unplanned pregnancy remains. Jeanne Lindsay's widely acclaimed book, *Pregnant Too Soon: Adoption Is an Option,* has helped young women face this crisis. Her *Open Adoption: A Caring Option* has helped them explore the option of open adoption, as well as the agencies and intermediaries offering this innovative service.

Parents, Pregnant Teens and the Adoption Option focuses on the often forgotten and neglected participants in the pregnancy – the extended family, particularly the birthgrandparents (the pregnant young woman's parents and the young father's parents). While an unplanned pregnancy is certainly a crisis for the birthmother, it is also a crisis for the whole family.

The pregnant teen's parents must come to terms with their own feelings regarding the pregnancy (such as guilt) and adoption. (Can they handle "giving up" their first grandchild?) It is normal for parents to feel guilty or somehow responsible for their daughter's pregnancy. They question how they failed, and wonder if something is wrong with them if they do not want to parent the baby themselves.

Counseling helps them deal with these very normal feelings.
This book gives the reader an opportunity to view teen pregnancy from the point of view of the family, and it will be
important reading for relatives and friends of anyone experiencing an unplanned pregnancy. Birthgrandparents will particularly
appreciate the opportunity to learn of the feelings and
experiences of others who have been in the same situation.

Traditionally, adoption agencies have focused on the child
and what is in the "best interest of the child," noting that the
child is their primary client. Counseling (which has typically
been minimal) has been offered to the birthmother, but usually
the birthfather has been ignored and the extended family
excluded.

Today, progressive adoption counselors recognize the importance of professional counseling for all parties. They offer
counseling not only for birthparents, but also for birthgrandparents to help them deal with their own crisis and pain and to
involve them in the adoption plan. Responsible adoption counselors also help birthparents explore all options (not just adoption), so they can be sure adoption is a decision with which
they can live.

In addition, it is important for adoption counselors to recognize that adoption is a grief experience, and to offer post-
placement counseling to help birthparents and their parents deal
with the normal feelings of grief. Unfortunately, some adoption
agencies and independent adoption services only offer counseling up to the point of legal relinquishment or consent; they are
not available to offer the important grief counseling afterward.
As mentioned, their services may be focused on the child, not
the birthparents.

I encourage adoption intermediaries to recognize the importance of the birthfamily in the adoption plan, and to make a
commitment to providing counseling and other services for
birthgrandparents. I encourage adoption professionals to offer
support groups for birthparents (such as an ongoing group which
meets once a month), as well as support groups for birthgrandparents. There are many innovative services such as support
groups and post-adoption services which can and should be

offered to better meet the needs of birthfamilies and adoptive families, and to help prepare them for the lifelong experience of adoption.

Typically, traditional adoption agencies exhibit a lot of control, making most of the decisions surrounding the adoption. On the other hand, progressive adoption intermediaries (agency or independent) allow the birthparents to make their own adoption plan. The control is in the birthparent's hands, rather than in the intermediary's hands. I am convinced this is healthier for all parties, both at the time a decision is made, and over the years of living with the decision.

I have personally been involved in the field of adoption for 20 years and was a pioneer in the practice of open adoption. I believe that open adoption (sharing identifying information, meeting in person, and having ongoing contact over the years) is more responsive to the needs of all parties, as well as healthier, than traditional adoption. In addition to the many benefits in open adoption for the birthparents (quicker resolution of grief, peace of mind about the adoption, and access to ongoing contact and information about the child), there are also benefits for the birthgrandparents and other extended family members. This form of adoption allows them to meet with and feel positive about the family who will be raising the child, and perhaps to have ongoing contact over the years with the child.

I applaud Jeanne Lindsay for helping the reader to explore and understand the experience of the birthfamily and the kinds of services which are helpful in dealing with all of the complex emotions involved. The very real and poignant stories, written by birthfamilies, which she has included will put the reader in touch with the emotions and feelings which result from an unplanned pregnancy.

This book is important reading for birthfamilies as well as adoption professionals. I hope it will help birthfamilies realize that they are not alone, and that other families have similar experiences and feelings.

I also hope this book will help birthfamilies demand counseling services and (if adoption is their choice) some involvement in the adoption process. In addition, I hope *Parents, Pregnant*

Teens and the Adoption Option will help adoption professionals become more sensitive to the needs of birthfamilies and, as a result, develop more responsive and innovative services for their clients.

Kathleen Silber, MSW
Co-author, *Dear Birthmother*
Associate Director, Independent Adoption Center
Pleasant Hill, California

ACKNOWLEDGMENTS

The birthgrandparents who shared their experiences so freely with me are the real authors of this book. I am grateful to all of them for their honesty and their openness as they discussed a difficult topic. Talking with them made my life richer, and I am deeply grateful. I would like to thank each one publicly, but I promised them complete anonymity. Their stories are changed slightly for this reason, but their experiences and their feelings are reported here as they shared them, in their words, not mine.

Two delightful birthgrandparents I can thank publicly are Jim and Judy Glynn, authors of the beautiful journal reprinted in this book. They are lovely, caring people, and they write well.

Several adoption counselors were especially helpful in referring birthgrandparents to me and in sharing their expertise gained from many years of working with birthparents and birthgrandparents. These include Claire Priester, Counselor, House of Ruth Ministries, Calvary Chapel, Downey, California; Jennifer Stebbins, Adoption Program Supervisor, Christian Adoption and Family Services, Anaheim, California; Sharon Kaplan, Executive Director, Parenting Resources, Tustin, California; Bonnie Adkins-DeJong, Director, and Jean Kennedy, Counselor, Bethany Christian Services, Bellflower, California;

John Holzhuter, Director, and Ruth Santner, Counselor, Catholic
Social Service, Topeka, Kansas.

Among the many other adoption professionals who shared
their expertise with me were Mary Struck, Director, Hope
Services, Seattle, Washington; Janet Cravins, Regional Director,
Lutheran Social Service, Corpus Christi, Texas; Marge Driscoll,
Birthparent Worker, Holy Family Services, Los Angeles,
California; Catherine Monserrat, Family Therapist, Seattle,
Washington; and Sr. Maureen Joyce, Executive Director, Com-
munity Maternity Services, Albany, New York. I also deeply
appreciate the "Foreword" written by Kathleen Silber, Associate
Director, Independent Adoption Center, Pleasant Hill,
California, and co-author of *Dear Birthmother*.

Julie Vetica, Teacher, School Age Mothers Program, La
Mirada, California, and Marge Eliason, Teacher/Counselor,
Young Families Program, Billings, Montana, gave me valuable
help with manuscript editing. Carole Blum provided day to day
encouragement, proof-reading assistance, and the expertise
and energy needed to keep our business going during book
writing time.

Tim Rinker designed the cover, Steve Lindsay of Action
Printing, Norman, Oklahoma, offered book layout guidance, and
Delta Lithograph printed *Parents, Pregnant Teens and the
Adoption Option*.

Bob, as always, was completely supportive while dealing
with the frantic schedule that writing this book required. It was
frantic because, when I finally started seriously working on
Parents, Pregnant Teens and the Adoption Option, I wanted it
done yesterday. He's a love.

INTRODUCTION

More than a million teenagers in the United States become pregnant each year. The majority didn't think it would happen to them.

These young people are not "those girls." They come from all kinds of homes and families. Some live in middle-class suburbs, others on farms, some in the "best" areas, others in inner-city slums.

Teenage pregnancy knows no socio-economic, ethnic, or religious barriers. It happens in traditional nuclear families, in blended families, and in single-parent families. It is happening in every community across America.

With more than a million teenage pregnancies, there are more than a million fathers, many of them teenagers themselves. They, too, are still dependent on their parents for a place to live, for financial and emotional support.

This book focuses more on the needs of pregnant teenage women and their parents than on the young men involved. However, many of these young men and their families need and deserve help too. If an adoption plan is being considered, the birthfather should be involved both from a legal standpoint and from his basic rights as a human being.

The young father's parents may be as upset about the pregnancy as are the young woman's parents. Several young fathers and their parents talk about their need for support as they share their experiences in this book.

Option – Single Parenthood

Many teenage women, with or without their partners, choose abortion as the "solution" to unplanned pregnancy. For most, this is not an easy decision. *There is no easy resolution for too-early pregnancy.*

For many teenagers, however, abortion is not an option. For religious, moral, and/or other personal reasons, she says, "I couldn't do that."

Three options remain: single parenthood, marriage, and adoption.

Single parenthood is difficult for mother and child even when the mother is an adult able to get and keep a well-paying job. If she is very young with no job skills and no high school diploma, she may expect her life to be difficult for a number of years.

To succeed as a single mother, she needs support – a place to live and adequate care for her child while she continues her education and/or works to support that child. She needs to have goals for her life, and she needs financial and emotional support, good health, and lots of guts to achieve those goals.

Many young mothers remain in their parents' homes, at least until they are adults. Three generations living in one household is often a difficult situation. Being someone's child at the same time she is someone's mother is complicated. Who is in charge? Who has the ultimate responsibility for the baby? Must the young mother still conform to her parents' rules? There are no easy answers in most families.

Teens Parenting: The Challenge of Babies and Toddlers is a parenting book written especially for very young parents. It is based on interviews with many teenage parents, and their comments reinforce the concepts presented on nutrition, bonding, discipline, and the many other topics relevant to the first two years of parenthood. Emphasis is on young parents who must live with their parents for awhile after their child is born.

Is Marriage an Option?

Marriage for young people not yet ready to support themselves is not likely to be much of an improvement over single parenthood. If the father is also a teenager, he probably needs more time to continue his education and to become job-ready. The pressure of dropping some of his goals in order to support his family may be tremendous.

But for many young fathers, the pressure created by going to work before they are ready is a luxury. They cannot find jobs.

There are other reasons teenage marriage has so little chance of succeeding. Young people change more rapidly during this stage of their lives than they ever will again. A young couple does not necessarily change in the same direction. Conceiving a child together at 16 does not mean they will have a good relationship when they are 30, 20, or even 17.

If the father is older and settled into a good job, the marriage may appear to have a good chance. Often, however, the young wife grows tired of her dependency. As she "grows up," she finds she needs an equal relationship, not another father.

For these and other reasons, the majority of teenage marriages fail. Getting married does not solve the problem of too-early pregnancy. See *Teenage Marriage: Coping with Reality* and *Teens Look at Marriage: Rainbows, Roles and Reality* (Morning Glory Press).

Teenage Marriage is written for young couples considering marriage or already living together while *Teens Look at Marriage* is an account of the research behind *Teenage Marriage*. The books are based on interviews with young couples already married or living together as teenagers, and on a cross-country survey of more than 3000 teenagers' attitudes toward and expectations of marriage.

The Other Option – Adoption

Parents, Pregnant Teens and the Adoption Option is about the other option, the option chosen by less than five percent of pregnant, unmarried teenagers. Adoption is not an easy solution either. In fact, when an adoption plan is made and carried out, it may seem to be the hardest decision of all. Parting with her baby

is difficult for the young birthmother, the birthfather, and both
birthfamilies.

Pregnant Too Soon: Adoption Is an Option (Morning Glory
Press), first published in 1980 and revised in 1988, is a book
about adoption written especially for young people. Young
women who were, by their own admission, "pregnant too soon,"
tell their stories. Most made the unpopular decision to release
for adoption, and they share their reasons for doing so. In
addition, the legal aspects of adoption including fathers' rights,
and vignettes of adoptive families and adoptees are included in
Pregnant Too Soon.

Birthgrandparents – grandparents whose grandchild has been
adopted into another family – are often deeply involved in
helping their daughter cope with too-early pregnancy. If she and
the young father-to-be consider an adoption plan, both sets of
parents need to be involved. How do they deal with the pain of
the early pregnancy and the possible continuing hurt of the
grandchild not remaining in their families? Many birthgrandparents share their experiences in the chapters which follow.

Over and over, they talk about the pain involved in the
decision-making process of considering an adoption plan for
their grandchild. They emphasize that the decision must be made
by the young birthparents. They stress the importance of providing support for the young parent whether the baby stays in the
family or is released to adoptive parents.

These birthgrandparents talk about the emotions they felt
when their grandchild was born and they held him/her in their
arms. If an adoption decision had been made, the hospital
experience was indeed bittersweet. The baby was theirs for only
a few days before going to the adoptive parents.

They stress the pain birthparents feel as they hold their baby,
knowing it is for such a brief time. Often the grandparents are so
intent on supporting their daughter's (or son's) grief that they
don't expect to grieve themselves. Many, however, found their
own grief to be overwhelming.

Often when a book includes extensive quotations from a
group of people, these quotes are printed in italics. Because the
voices of the birthgrandparents are the most important part of

this book, however, their words are in standard type. Explanatory material including quotes from adoption professionals are printed in italics.

Adoption in the United States today is seldom the closed, absolutely secret event which was typical a generation or two ago. Most adoption agencies attempt to honor the preferences the birthparent(s) express for adoptive parents for their child. More and more across the country birthparents choose the adoptive couple from a group of resumes which often include photographs of the would-be adoptive parents.

In some areas, adoption agencies and independent adoption services offer meetings between the birth- and adoptive parents, and some suggest continued contact between the two families. "Cooperative adoption" refers to an adoption plan worked out cooperatively between the birth- and adoptive families. At this time, there is no legal power for the birthparents in this kind of arrangement. The adoptive parents are the parents both from a legal standpoint and on a day-to-day parenting basis, but the birthparents and birthgrandparents may be known to the child and may be part of his life.

The birthgrandparents interviewed for this book represent a wide range of adoption planning from closed to cooperative. Whatever the degree of openness discussed, the need for counseling for both birth- and adoptive families is stressed.

Most of the grandparents who share their experiences on these pages felt terribly alone during their daughters' pregnancies. They hope their comments may help others facing the dilemma of a young daughter facing pregnancy too soon.

Sometimes adoption is the wisest choice for the baby and for the birthparents. It's never an easy choice.

Counseling for Teens, Parents

Adoption counselors know how important it is for a teenager considering an adoption plan to have the support of her/his parents. Legally, the adoption decision is made solely by the birthmother and the birthfather.

However, even if a teenage birthmother would like to consider adoption because she wants more for her child than she can provide, she may be stopped by parents who say, "You can't give our baby away." Sometimes this happens in the hospital immediately after delivery.

The young mother, especially if she is planning to release her child through an adoption agency, has probably received regular counseling help. Perhaps she has seriously considered her desires for her baby and knows she will grieve, but has decided to place him with another family.

Her parents, however, are far less likely to be involved in counseling. The young father's parents are even less apt to be offered help in dealing with their feelings concerning the pregnancy and the possible adoption planning. If your young daughter is pregnant or your teenage son has caused a pregnancy, you may already have helped her/him find counseling help. Whether or not s/he is considering an adoption plan, seeking help in dealing with the crisis of early pregnancy is wise. This kind of help is usually available through adoption agencies even if the young couple are quite certain they will rear their child themselves.

If they are considering adoption, it is still imperative they look at all their options and *make a decision.* Either keeping the baby or releasing for adoption should not be an "of course" situation. Each of the baby's parents needs seriously to consider all the options before making a decision. For this reason, it's best either to contact a licensed adoption agency or an independent adoption service which offers counseling to its clients. A few adoption attorneys also insist on counseling for their birthparent and adoptive parent clients.

Not all adoption agencies and independent adoption services provide counseling for the families of birthparents. In fact, not many do at this time. Or they may have counseling available, but don't broadcast the fact. If you ask about it, however, you may be able to get help for yourself as well as for your daughter or son. Ideally, you and your teenager will work with different counselors.

Whether or not you utilize professional counseling services, the experiences shared on these pages by birthgrandparents may help you cope with the trauma of a too-early pregnancy in your family.

1

THE REVELATION – SHE'S PREGNANT!

"When Becky told me she was pregnant, I thought my world had come to an end. Excuse me if I start crying, but I think it's all over and here I go again. (Lucia, mother of 15-year-old Becky.)

More than a million teenagers become pregnant each year in the United States. Nearly 500,000 give birth. But the fact that it's happening in other families doesn't make it easy to accept if it's my daughter – or yours.

"Not my daughter!" Pregnancy only happens to "those girls," young women without goals in families without plans for the future. That's what many of us think. But too-early pregnancy hits all ethnic groups at all socio-economic levels. With nearly half of all 16-year-olds sexually active today, pregnancy is the result for many young women. Many young men, too, become fathers before they're ready to parent.

If it's your daughter who says those fateful words, "I'm

pregnant," what do you do? Do you panic? Do you cry? Do you throw her out?

Most of us as parents react with shock, with hurt, and with the knowledge that our daughter needs our support now more than ever before.

NOT OUR DAUGHTER!

Georgia had worked on the hot line in a Crisis Pregnancy Center. She had heard the hurt and the pain which so often results from too-early pregnancy, but she didn't expect it in her family.

"When someone in your own family tells you she's pregnant, it's such a feeling of helplessness," she observed. "You can't help as much because you're directly involved." Georgia continued talking about her daughter, Lilia, 16:

My first reaction was anger. How could Lilia do this to us?

We were going skiing that day. Lilia didn't want to go, but we said, "You're going." I think she was being punished for something and we weren't going to leave her home by herself.

An hour before we were to leave, Lilia said, "Mom, please sit down. I want to tell you something." I probably sighed because I was rushing around getting ready to leave.

As I sat down, Lilia blurted, "Mom, I think I'm pregnant."

I told Lilia to go upstairs. My husband had just gotten out of the shower, and I said, "We've got to talk *now*." He pulled on his pants and we went out to the garage. I hadn't exploded or even cried yet.

Like most men, Eric isn't very emotional or expressive. He didn't cry, but he held me while I did. Then we went back into our bedroom. We were devastated, and we lay on our bed for a couple of hours.

We finally called Lilia downstairs. I don't know what agony she'd gone through during those two hours. Eric told

her we had trusted her, and she had violated that trust.
Then he broke down and sobbed.

We realized what a blow this would be to our families.
We more or less closed down shop that day. We closed the
doors and didn't go anywhere.

Actually that went on for a couple of weeks. We'd go to
work but it was low-profile. We didn't talk much to
anybody during that time. We couldn't because we'd have
started crying if we had.

I couldn't believe that my daughter. . .she'd been seeing
this boy for three years, and I'd told her over and over to
break it off, that she was too young to see only one boy.

They'd spend time with each other's families, watch
TV at his house or ours, but we hadn't allowed her to have
real dates at all until she was 16, and by then she was a
month pregnant.

Our Worst Fear Is Realized

*Donna and Curtis were concerned that Yvonne, 16, and
Brian, also 16, were becoming too close in their relationship.
The teenagers had been dating nearly a year when Donna and
Curtis' worst fears were realized last year:*

I guess it was in February – Yvonne was a senior in high
school – and we got word that she wasn't going to school.
Both Curtis and I have to leave before Yvonne and her
brother get up, so we didn't know she wasn't going.

After we found out, we confronted her with it. She said,
"Well, I haven't felt good lately and I can't get up . . ."

We said, "Well, you need to go to the doctor and see if
anything is wrong."

I left the next day on a business trip and was spending
the night in L.A., so my sister Claudia went to the doctor
with Yvonne. Somehow in my heart I knew what it was.
That whole day it was like a panic inside me.

When I got to the hotel room that night, I called home.
Curtis didn't know anything other than Yvonne had gone
to the doctor, and that she was over at Claudia's. I called

her there and asked, "How was the doctor visit? What did she say?"

"Oh nothing. She wants me to come back for some tests." Yvonne has a hard time confronting difficult issues.

"Yvonne, are you telling me the whole truth? Let me talk to Claudia."

"Claudia, what did she say?" I asked.

"I think Yvonne needs to tell you," she replied. At that point I knew, and it was like total panic. I just couldn't believe it. Was this really happening to us?

So I said, "Claudia, tell me."

"Yvonne's pregnant," she said.

I was on the sixth floor of the hotel sitting on the bed looking out the window. Instantly the thought went through my head, "Just jump." I began to cry out to the Lord, "Lord, why? It can't be, it can't be." I had forgotten to take my Bible with me, and, thank God, there was a Gideon Bible there. I opened it and started to read the Twenty-third Psalm.

The next day I had to be at this job fair, and I felt I couldn't do it. I was the only one representing the company so, after a sleepless night, I went to the job fair, stayed half a day, shut it down, and went home.

When I got home, Curtis and I went into our bedroom. I said, "We have a problem we need to talk about." After I told him, we went into the living room, and Yvonne just sat there, looking scared and alone.

What do you do? You deal with it. By that time Yvonne and Brian had broken up, and nobody else knew. Brian didn't even know, we learned later.

Sometimes She Doesn't Tell

A teenager is likely to keep her pregnancy a secret as long as possible. If she doesn't want to be pregnant, she may subconsciously feel, "If I don't think about it, perhaps it will go away." She may be afraid to tell her parents.

From a health standpoint, not acknowledging her pregnancy is unwise. A pregnant woman of whatever age needs to see her doctor early in her pregnancy. Because teenage pregnancy is high-risk, very young women especially need to check with their doctors as soon as possible after conception has occurred. If she doesn't admit she's pregnant, she misses out on this important early medical care.

Most pregnant teenagers need to make some changes in their life-style in order to deliver a healthy baby. Smoking, drinking alcohol, and taking drugs, of course, are all no-nos during pregnancy.

Nutrition is an extremely important part of producing a healthy baby. Teenagers who insist they do just fine with a lunch of french fries and cola need to make a big change in their eating habits during pregnancy.

Parents can help their daughter understand the importance of good prenatal care – if they know she's pregnant. For many, the months go by without that knowledge. Alice and Tom didn't learn of Roseanne's pregnancy until six weeks before their grandchild was born:

Roseanne was dating Doug, and he seemed to isolate her. Roseanne is a very social person, not a loner. She loves people and has to have people around her. She doesn't like to do anything by herself. But after she and Doug started going together, she began to draw away from other people.

We've learned since that Doug was quite jealous. When they were here at home, they were very physical with each other, touching each other as they shouldn't have. We talked to Roseanne about it, but at that point in her life her attitude was very different from what it is now. She would look at us like, "I hear you but you're wasting your breath." This went on for quite a while. They went together for over a year.

Roseanne and Doug still denied she was pregnant.

I had suspected Roseanne was pregnant although she never showed it in the way most women show. Several times I asked, "Roseanne, are you pregnant?"

"No, no, no."

There was a time that year at winter camp she was frightened, and she shared with another boy in her youth group that she thought she was pregnant. This was several months before we knew it.

Through a chain of events, it went through the youth group and to the pastor. Several of the kids involved in spreading the rumor met with the pastor. Roseanne and Doug still denied that she was pregnant.

Time went on, and in June we were visiting some friends. We were all out by the pool playing, but Roseanne just sat there.

She wouldn't put a bathing suit on, and it was like the Lord finally said to me, "She's pregnant." Her body was different, but she didn't look like a pregnant woman. She simply looked like she was gaining weight.

> *My heart broke for her,*
> *and we cried a lot.*

We'd gone to our friend's house in two cars, so Roseanne and I came back together. I knew I had to confront her, and I had to do it before we got home. Saying we were stopping for something, I pulled off under a shade tree and said, "Roseanne, are you pregnant?" She started to sob.

My heart broke for her, and we cried a lot. She was still going with Doug, and I said, "Well, what are you two going to do?"

We talked for an hour. She told me she had already decided to place the baby for adoption. I said, "Have you been to a doctor?"

"No."

This was six weeks before Shauna was born, and Roseanne had never seen a doctor. We came home, and I went in the bedroom and told Roseanne's father. He was absolutely shocked. He had no idea anything was wrong other than Roseanne was gaining weight.

Actually it was easy for Roseanne to conceal the baby. She's a tall girl and she likes to wear baggy clothes. And she hadn't gained a lot of weight.

What About the Father?

So often the teenage father-to-be is forgotten. If his parents are involved at all, it may be only to pay the bills. Intense feelings concerning the pregnancy are usually credited to the pregnant teenager and her family, not to the boy and his family as well.

Doug's parents, however, were also dealing with tremendous shock and disappointment when they learned of Roseanne's pregnancy. Doug's mother, Ginny, talked about it:

It's a lot harder than I thought. I'm not a good person to be in touch with my feelings. Neither is my family.

I had been worried about Doug and Roseanne's relationship because of the hours and their obvious closeness. I had spoken to both of them, but of course they said, "Oh no, no problem." Being from a very strong moral Christian ethic, my husband and I both feel that sex before marriage is just not an option, so the fear of that was awful.

There was a rumor in the youth group at our church that Roseanne and Doug were sexually involved, and they were brought before the pastor. They said she wasn't pregnant.

One hot day a few weeks later, they came into the house, and I could tell from the way Roseanne walked that, yes, she was pregnant. I took my son out and said, "Roseanne is pregnant, isn't she?"

He said, "Yes."

Our disappointment was tremendous, and my husband is still dealing with that, just that our child could do that, go against all that we held sacred, and that he'd been taught was sacred. Some people accept this, know that the sexual encounters are going on. But we feel so strongly that this is not what God has planned for us. The awful disappointment and the hurt, and, of course, anger comes in there. You could kill, maim, and mutilate at any moment.

But the sanity returns, and you think about what needs
to be done. Roseanne's support from her family made it
easier for us. Doug continued to be involved constantly
throughout the pregnancy.

"We've Failed Her. . ."

*Often parents feel they must have failed their daughter if she
becomes pregnant. They feel guilty and think they must not have
been good parents. "Where did we go wrong?" they ask their
daughters. Lucia, mother of Becky, 17, is still having trouble
dealing with her guilt feelings:*

The first thing Becky told me was that she was getting
an abortion in two days. I was in a state of shock because
her father and I don't believe in abortion, and I knew she
didn't either. I went to the phone and called everyone I
could think of, adoption agencies, counselors, our minister.

Within two days Becky decided against abortion. From
there she went into counseling. Would she keep the baby
or place it for adoption? At that time, before we knew she
was pregnant, she was pretty rebellious toward her father
and me. We said we could keep the baby, but she didn't
like that.

One of my first feelings was that I was a failure as a
mother. For that matter, I still do. I haven't come to grips
with that. You raise a child for 17 years and you think,
"This is the end result. I've done a lot of things wrong. My
daughter is pregnant, and there is nothing I can do to
change that. I can't go back."

Becky doesn't seem to feel that way. Neither does my
husband. He's always trying to cheer me up by saying,
"You didn't do it." Becky, of course, gets exasperated
when I try to talk to her about it.

"You didn't get pregnant, Mom. I did," she says.

The whole morality issue – I certainly wasn't an angel
as a teenager, but how you deal with sex as a teenager
today is very different. There *is* a morality issue. I've tried
not to moralize, but it's still there. I realize she's not the

first girl in the world to get pregnant, nor will she be the last. But somehow, because she's intelligent and has high goals, I didn't think it would happen to her.

Sometimes I say to her, "I can understand that you have different morals than I do, but I can't understand why you were so stupid." Was she sleeping in health class when they talked about birth control? She said she thought she was having sex at her safe time. . .

She was only a month pregnant when she told me. I'm sure she was scared and had to tell someone. Her relationship with the baby's father was very short-term. He offered to marry her, but it would never have worked, and Becky basically never gave it a thought. She figured this was not an option.

Expressing Feelings Is Difficult

Often parents deny their own pain, their own feelings, according to Sharon Kaplan, Parenting Resources, Tustin, California. "I see so many unexpressed feelings. They're afraid they'll upset their daughter." Fathers, especially, tend not to be able to express their feelings, according to Kaplan. "Many find it difficult to push past the anger and get to the grief," she concluded.

"Sometimes I hear from women, 'He's angry, and he won't talk to me.' That often leads to marital stress," Kaplan added.

Karen's grandfather and two uncles were ministers, and Karen, 15, was attending a private church school. Perhaps this was partly why her father had such a difficult time accepting her pregnancy. He didn't talk much, but Cynthia, Karen's mother, shared their story:

How do you feel when you find out? It's hard to describe. For myself and Bob, there was a lot of anger, there's no getting around that. You think, this can't be true. That's the first thing that hits you. How can this possibly be happening to us?

You think you just read about it in the paper, all these statistics, and that your kids aren't going to be part of the statistics. That's what you're sure to say at first, "This can't be true."

I don't think we dealt with it the best. How do you prepare? I know we weren't prepared. I'm not saying it's any easier for other people than it was for us, but with my husband's brothers and father being ministers, and we're part of a closed community with Karen going to a private school. . .

I waver back and forth. I've always been pretty independent. Who cares what they think? That's what got me through. I had to deal with it on a personal level, not thinking about anyone else.

I thought I'd failed, that somehow
I'd done something wrong, and I'd failed.

I spent days crying and crying. I kept flashing back to when the kids were little, and I thought I could protect them from everything. I guess that's one of the things we've had to work through.

We had to realize Karen's 15, she's getting older, she has to make decisions for herself. We can't always be there telling her, "This is what you should do, and this is what you should not do."

Somehow I thought I'd failed, that somehow I'd done something wrong, and I'd failed. I know that's not true, but I had to work through that. *(She's crying as she talks.)*

I also had to deal with the whole idea of abortion. I know what my religion and my church say, but I don't necessarily agree.

The first thing we could think was, "You have to have an abortion." How can a 15-year-old have a baby? I have to say for Karen — she was adamantly opposed to abortion, and in retrospect, I'm glad she was.

That was a terrible, terrible time, and I think maybe she saved us from having a harder time living with something worse (the abortion) than what we live with now. There's a lot of pain still, but there is some joy. The other way, there would have been nothing good.

This whole thing is something I still have to live with, but at the same time I can't sit here and condemn people who make the choice of abortion. I would be lying if I said otherwise. It's something each person has to deal with individually.

Early on we called a counselor from our church. I didn't know her – we just talked on the phone. "My daughter is so immature in some respects. There is no way she can parent this child," I said.

"Maybe this will be the catalyst for Karen to mature, to make her grow up," she replied. And I'm thinking, how can we use this baby as a possibility that Karen might grow up? That didn't seem right to me to take that chance. Who loses then? If Karen doesn't grow up, the baby is the loser.

Then the lady started talking about money. That turned me off. You're feeling absolutely terrible and she talks about money. I never called her back. Karen got a counselor's name from someone at school, and she started going there. After a while we went there, too, for counseling. In fact, we've become good friends with the counselor.

How Can Friends Help?

Over and over birthgrandparents talked about their feelings of being alone. Sometimes they wanted to be left alone for awhile. Others needed to talk and didn't know where to go. Sometimes they encountered people who made hurtful comments. Others realized months later that their friends had wanted to help but didn't know how. Cynthia continued her story:

I didn't want to share with friends back then. In fact, I couldn't tell anyone. We were very angry at Karen, and we told her, "You have to tell people. You have hurt so many people, you have to tell them. You tell Grandma and Grandpa." It was hard, but she did. It was not a nice thing to do, but I can't deny what we felt.

The very next day my sister came, and I love my sister, but I didn't want to see anyone. Then my sister-in-law came over. I said, "Why did you come? I don't feel like talking to anybody."

You waver back and forth. Sometimes I was so ashamed, so embarrassed. . .I couldn't talk to anyone. That's probably not the right attitude, but that's the way one thinks.

Karen didn't choose the abortion route because she thought it was wrong, and she was strong enough to take all the pressure, the cruelty, the ostracism, to stick up for what she believed in. Would I have been strong enough to do that? I don't know. I might not have.

There's a woman at church who I used to know in high school. She came up to me one Sunday and said, "How's your daughter doing?"

I said, "Which one?" (Karen has two younger sisters.)

She didn't even know Karen's name, so she said, "The one that had the baby." I should have told her it was none of her business.

She proceeded to tell me she didn't know why Karen didn't keep the baby. And she went on to tell me about her brother in Colorado who had sent her the news. She's saying how could this be, this sweet little girl with the pony tail playing Bobbie Sox. I don't usually even talk to her at church, and she simply came over to get the story. That bugged me.

That kind of person I don't appreciate. I think that for something this personal, people should not intrude. I really had to be left alone. That's how I had to deal with it. I felt so bad, and I knew they wouldn't understand.

You have a whole life ahead of you to do things, to feel good about yourself.

Bob and I got to the point where we'd say, "Nuts with people. It's done with. We can't change it, so let's live with it day to day." It's not easy.

I told Karen that a lot of times. "Don't hang your head. When you walk out the door, hold your head up. So you made a mistake, a tragic mistake that you have to live with,

but your life isn't over. You have a whole life ahead of you
to do things, to feel good about yourself."

The person I appreciated the most was the friend who
sent me a note in the mail. All she said was, "If you need
anything, just let me know. If you need somebody to watch
the kids so you and Bob can get away, let me know. I'm
thinking of you." That was all. That was what I appreciated. Just don't be intrusive. Maybe she knew because her
husband was killed a few years ago. Maybe she realized
that for awhile you have to be let alone to deal with what
you have to deal with.

Emotional Support Is Crucial

*Unlike Cynthia, some people need to share their problems
with others. Mary Lou, mother of Stacy, 16, talked about getting
emotional support from friends and relatives:*

A teenage daughter's pregnancy is a touchy subject, but
most of the people we know are aware of our situation.
Most of our friends were supportive. They were willing to
talk about it with us, but they didn't try to push us into
conversation.

A few friends called or wrote to Stacy to express
concern, to tell her they were proud of her for going
through this pregnancy, and that they loved her.

In the beginning parents go through tremendous emotional upsets. First you're shocked, you're disappointed,
you're angry. What did we do wrong? What could we have
done to prevent this? You go through all these emotions in
the beginning.

When you finally come to grips with the fact that you
have a pregnant daughter, you start accepting it. The most
important thing is to learn to communicate with one
another, husband with wife, parent with child. We told her
we loved her, and we shared the fact that we were disappointed, that we were angry. We assured her that we would
support her and be here to help her with her decision.

Stacy was almost five months pregnant before we knew.
She told only her boyfriend and a girlfriend. They were her
support during those five months.

She finally told me one night, and I told her dad. He
talked with her little brother so he wouldn't feel left out.
Next we went to our parents, our brothers and sisters, and
our friends. I think you need a support group for yourself.
Perhaps you don't want to broadcast it to everybody, but
you need friends to help keep it in the open. You don't post
a big sign on the front porch, "My daughter is pregnant,"
but you need to talk.

Some people may not react the way you want – "I told
you something would happen." You have to be ready to
take that. You have already accused yourself, you already
feel guilty. So if they come at you with that, don't be
shocked. Just let them express their feelings just as you
have. After the hostilities are out, say, "Where do we go
from here?"

She Needs Your Support

*No matter how hurt, how shocked, how devastated parents
feel when they learn their daughter is pregnant or their son has
caused a pregnancy, they usually realize the importance of
supporting and caring for that daughter or that son in the heavy
decisions which must be faced. If this is happening to you, your
daughter – or your son – needs you now more than ever before.*

Anne spoke for most parents when she said:

Joan was ashamed. She thought I'd think less of her.
When she learned I could accept it, that I wasn't going
to condemn her, that I'd give her the support she
needed, I think it helped. What possible good can it do
to condemn? It doesn't get anyone anywhere, and your
child can be scarred for life. This pregnancy was something we couldn't avoid after it happened, and I wasn't
about to destroy her life because she made a mistake.

2

COPING WITH REALITY – AND MOVING ON

Many parents find it difficult to accept their teenager's pregnancy. After a little time to adjust to the shock, they know there are things to do, doctor's appointments to be made, counseling to be considered. Will she continue to live at home? What about school? How do we tell our friends? Our parents? The list seems endless.

Consider Practical Issues

Ted and Mary Lou's daughter, Stacy, was an eleventh grader and head of her school's cheerleading squad. Both parents shared their reaction to the news of her pregnancy and the steps that must be taken soon:

Ted: I'm a practical type of guy. My first thought was, "We've got a problem. How do we fix it? What do we do? We have to do something immediately." So we started planning.

First, before we went to the doctor, I talked with Stacy.
I was hoping she'd tell me she had eaten too much or
something, that it wasn't real. After a couple of questions,
I knew it was real.

Stacy had already talked with a girl at school whose
sister had gone through a pregnancy, so she knew about
MediCal (state medical insurance). We started keeping a
list of the things we bought and the medical expenses –
which weren't very much once we got into MediCal.

> *We aren't out to get anyone,*
> *but both kids were scared,*
> *and we needed to talk about that.*

The baby's father doesn't have good communication
with his parents, and they didn't know. He was afraid to
tell them. He kept saying he would, but after three weeks, I
wrote them a letter. We hadn't met them, and I thought this
was the best way to do it. We aren't out to get anyone, but
both kids were scared, and we needed to talk.

His father called the next night, and we mostly talked
finances. He came over the next day and gave us a check
which covered most of the expenses we had.

We assumed first we'd raise the baby here. Then I
started thinking. I couldn't see how we could do that and
be fair to anybody.

I knew Stacy had to talk to somebody, and our minister
gave us some referrals. She mentioned two places, an
independent counseling center and an adoption agency. We
decided the agency was the place to go, and the three of us
went down to talk to them.

Everything we did was 1-2-3-4. We had to go to the
doctor. We had to see the father's parents. We had to get
MediCal. And then we had to get Stacy to a counseling
center.

Another thing we had to plan was who to tell and how to
tell them. We decided we'd talk to people close to us.
Mary Lou was having her 40th birthday party in two

weeks, and we didn't tell people before that. I told my sister first, and then I went to see my folks. It didn't surprise them as much as I expected. They'd noticed Stacy hadn't been acting like her old self. Two months earlier during Christmas we were talking about things we were thankful for, and what we were looking forward to. Stacy broke down and cried, and we didn't know why.

My family all agreed, "This is a shame, but we'll support you."

The next weekend we told our next door neighbors, and I also told my best friend. Of all these people we talked to, only two mentioned abortion, and one of them was my mother. The other was my best friend. When I told him Stacy wasn't going to do that, he said, "For heavens sake, why not?"

They have a son a year younger than Stacy, and they've grown up together. I know Stacy's pregnancy was a big shock to him.

Everybody kept telling us we were doing a great job of coping, but it was Stacy who really did the coping. She was the strong one. I'd been telling her since she was three years old, "Don't grow up too fast." Well, she grew up very fast, but now she's back to the business of being a teenager.

I told Stacy she should go to school and walk with her shoulders back.

From the time we knew, we realized we didn't want to hide anything. I told Stacy she should go to school and walk with her shoulders back. If someone stared at her, she should walk over and say, "What do you want to know?"

In the last three months, though, she became a little self-conscious. She felt awkward, especially around men, and didn't know what to say.

Stacy wanted to stay home a lot. It wasn't a problem to go out as a family, but we didn't visit people much or have people over here during that time.

Family Members Are Involved

*Brothers and sisters may react strongly to a too-early preg-
nancy in the family. Ted and Mary Lou were concerned about
their son's response to Stacy's pregnancy:*

Ted: It was hard for Steve, our 12-year-old son, to deal
with Stacy's pregnancy. He wasn't getting what he wanted
during those months because we spent so much time with
Stacy. We explained to him that his sister was going
through a bad time, that she had problems. It was hard for
him to understand.

Mary Lou: Especially my time. I was working, and
when I came home, if Stacy wanted to talk, we'd sometimes sit and talk for two hours. When Steve wanted to
talk, it had to be little bits of my time. He had trouble
understanding that Stacy needed that extra time.

Ted: Until the last month, Steve didn't want any of the
kids at school to know because he thought they'd give him
a bad time. He told Stacy that when any of his friends
came over, he wanted her to sit down or stay out of sight.
He didn't want his friends to know.

Mary Lou: He'd say, "How come you did something
stupid like that?" He didn't know what to say to the kids.
After Chris was born, Steve came to the hospital to see
Stacy, and he went to the nursery window to see Chris.

*Belinda, 13, was upset when she learned her brother Doug's
girlfriend, Roseanne, was pregnant. Belinda's mother, Beth,
explained:*

Belinda was very angry when she learned Doug's
girlfriend, Roseanne, was pregnant. Doug doesn't understand that. Soon after she realized what was happening,
Belinda told Doug, "I don't want you talking to her. I feel
like she's been hateful to you." That's not how I see it, but
Belinda had to put her anger somewhere.

Belinda went with us to the hospital to see the baby. She cried the whole night afterward because she didn't want to give the baby up. It's been difficult for her.

Birthgrandparents need to be sensitive to the needs of their other children while they're dealing with the pregnancy of their daughter or their son's girlfriend. Some adoption agencies and independent adoption services offer counseling to all members of the birthfamilies including siblings of the birthparents.

More Decisions to Make

Anne didn't know 13-year-old Joan was pregnant until very late. Joan had gone to a party one weekend when her mother was out of town. She drank too much, and scarcely understood what had happened.

It was three months before she realized, to her horror, that she might be pregnant. She talked to the young woman, a family friend, who had stayed with her the weekend her mother was gone. "I'll take care of it," she told Joan. But she never did.

Joan finally told her mother late one night. Joan's parents were divorced several years ago and rarely talked with each other. Anne knew her daughter needed immediate medical care, and she knew she had to tell Joan's father:

I never see him. He sends a check each month but that's all. The next morning I called him at 7 a.m. and said, "Your daughter is pregnant."

I called the doctor as soon as the office opened and said my child *had* to see a doctor that afternoon. We went in two hours later, and Joan's father and his wife met us there.

The doctor was so kind and understanding. His wife, who is a nurse-practitioner, works with him, and they helped us through this. First they gave Joan an ultrasound, then told us the baby was due in about five weeks – which I found almost impossible to believe. How could I be so naive?

Alice and Tom considered sending Roseanne to a maternity home during her pregnancy, but they changed their minds:

Alice: The wheels started in motion. We got her to the doctor, and we started doing the things that pregnant women do. At first Roseanne thought she might go away and not face her friends. She was still going to church. Up until now, only her boyfriend knew.

I got information about St. Anne's in Los Angeles. By this time we had shared the news with our immediate family, our brothers and sisters, and they were very supportive. My husband's younger sister, Sally, who has always been close to Roseanne, was especially helpful.

Sally and I talked about St. Anne's, and she said, "I hate to see her go to some strange place where she doesn't know anybody."

So Roseanne decided to stay at home. I think it was a comfort to her to be here. She needed the familiarity of her own surroundings during that time.

The Need to Talk

Counseling services are usually available for birthparents, but birthgrandparents may not be included. Catherine felt both she and daughter Donnette needed counseling:

I didn't go with Donnette to counseling because she went during the day and I work. I had no one to help me through my grief.

Of course the agency is designed to help the birthmother, but I felt cheated that no one was tuned in to my needs. My needs are also important and genuine.

I did see the counselor a couple of times, and she helped me a lot. I believe in counseling. I share because I feel good when I share. Having a pregnant daughter is difficult. I need to share.

Kate and her daughter were referred to Catholic Social Service in their midwestern town:

We all went in together the first time, Luanne, her father and his wife, my husband and me. Max (our counselor) talked with us for nearly two hours. He told us everything about their services and how adoption works.

Max said someone else would counsel Luanne, and that the rest of us could see him at any time. He said the counseling would be on the pros and cons of keeping the baby and of adoption. He explained why it was so important for Luanne to consider both keeping the baby and the adoption choice. She needed to look at both sides.

My husband and I went in several times to talk with Max, and I think it helped us cope. It wasn't easy.

The need to talk to someone about her daughter's pregnancy was also expressed by Georgia whose daughter, Lilia, was 16:

I needed somebody to talk to, but I don't work closely with anyone. A woman I see occasionally was friendly, so one day I said, "Jeanne, I've got to talk to you. Can we go somewhere?"

We went out to my car, and Jeanne said, "OK, what is it, Georgia?"

I started crying and burst out, "My daughter's pregnant."

To my horror, Jeanne laughed. She said, "I have a three-month-old baby at home, and my daughter is also 16."

"How did you get through it?" I asked. She talked a little, but mostly she listened. I needed that. I also needed to know it could happen in other families.

It's a real shocker when it happens to your own family, a rude awakening.

Because of this friendship, I've gotten involved with three women from our church. Two of them have pregnant teenage daughters, and the other one's daughter had a baby two months ago. I asked them if they'd like to come over and do some sharing. All three said they liked the idea.

I discovered you can have even worse problems. Two of them are having marriage difficulties. One husband

actually blames his wife for their daughter getting pregnant. Another one feels her daughter put her through all
this, but nobody cares how she feels.

We talked and shed a lot of tears. I was surprised at the
deep feelings that came out. It's a real shocker when it
happens to your own family, a rude awakening.

There is a grieving time now before the baby is born.

I think the big thing a family can do is be supportive.
My parents aren't supportive in this, and neither are my
husband's parents. A lot of our family members aren't, and
I'm shocked.

When we adopted Lilia, they accepted her with open
arms just as if we had given birth. Now they aren't supportive of her adoption plan, and that hurts. We're having to
separate ourselves from friends and relatives who don't
understand. It hurts that they don't even make an effort.

There is a grieving time now before the baby is born.
Today you caught me at one of my vulnerable moments. I
was having a good cry when you called. There are times
when I'm outstandingly brave and courageous, other times
I'm not at all.

For awhile you blame yourselves, and if you don't get
support from other people, it makes you feel worse.

*If your teenager is pregnant, or has caused a pregnancy, s/he
would undoubtedly profit from talking with a counselor. Adoption agency counselors are trained to help their clients look
carefully at **all** their options, and to consider the consequences
of each possible decision.*

*When you're learning about counseling services available for
your teenager, ask about help for yourself. You may find you'd
like assistance in dealing with your own feelings as well as the
specifics of providing support for your teenager.*

*To find counseling help, look in the yellow pages of your
telephone book under "Adoption Services," "Human Services*

Organizations," "Marriage, Family and Child Counselors,"
"Social Service Organizations," and other similar headings.

Importance of School

*School is an important part of most teenagers' lives. Schools
used to expel students who became pregnant. (Was pregnancy
contagious? How else could we have justified denying an
education to an expectant mother?)*

*No longer is this legal in public schools. Title IX, Guidelines
of the Education Amendments of 1972, requires equal educational opportunities for women in every state. It forbids sex dis-
crimination in any educational institution receiving federal
assistance. This includes all public schools and many private
institutions.*

*Title IX states that a school cannot keep any student from
participating in a class or extracurricular activity because of the
student's pregnancy or marital status.*

*Catherine knew how important it was that Donnette stay
in school:*

The school would have provided a tutor for three
months, but I didn't go along with that because the school
wasn't responsible for Donnette's pregnancy. I felt
strongly that if she was physically able, she should be in
school.

Donnette could have transferred to an alternative school,
but she chose to stay where she was. I'm 42, and when I
was in high school, pregnant girls were kicked out. I
assumed Donnette couldn't stay, and I was concerned about
that. I went over to talk to her counselor to see what we
needed to do so Donnette could continue school
somewhere.

The counselor was startled at my question, and she said,
"Donnette can come to school. There are 17 others here
who are pregnant."

Donnette made a poor decision, and I have always
taught her she must accept the consequences of her decisions. I wanted her to be in charge of her life, and she
handled it remarkably well. She took a certain amount of

flack from some people, but that was mostly when they
learned she was making an adoption plan.

If your daughter is attending public school and the counselor
suggests she should drop out, ask to speak to the Title IX admin-
istrator in your school district. Your daughter has every right to
continue attending school throughout her pregnancy and as
soon after delivery as she's able. A doctor's permit to return to
class should not be required by the school unless a similar
permit is required for students with other temporary disabilities.

But many pregnant teenagers still drop out of school. Per-
haps she feels awkward, or she doesn't fit in the desk. She may
have the choice of attending an alternative program for preg-
nant students. According to Title IX, the school must not insist
she leave her regular classes to attend a special program.

If you aren't aware of such a program, call your school
district office and ask about services for pregnant students. If a
special program is available, suggest to your daughter that you
go together to check it out. She may prefer to stay in her regular
school, but the more choices she feels she has, the better
decisions she's likely to make.

Private School Expels Her

Cynthia also realized the importance of school to her tenth
grade daughter. Karen, because she was not attending public
school, was expelled because of her pregnancy:

Karen was going to a private Christian school, and she
got kicked out suddenly when they heard she was pregnant.
She was bitter about that. It bothered me a lot, too. If
you're 15 and pregnant, you feel pretty much like an
outcast anyway, and you don't need people to act like
you're contagious.

Karen stayed home for two weeks, and she needed to be
in school. She needed to be doing what she would nor-
mally be doing. I think those two weeks added tremendous
pressure to all of us. The people at her school have no idea
what their kicking her out did to all of us.

They changed their policy a year later, but it's not going to be easy for other girls. They still have people there with their old ideas, and they think a pregnant girl ought to be punished.

They may let her stay in school, but the way they look at her or the way a teacher talks to her. . .I'm not blaming people – it's just something that will take a while.

Karen has high aspirations – she wants to be a lawyer. She didn't want to go to the pregnant girls' school because she didn't think it would be a challenge. They finally admitted her to the district's college-prep school.

It didn't matter to the principal that she was pregnant.

The counselor and the kids there were good about it. Karen missed her own school a lot, but she did well there. In fact, she got the outstanding math student award that year. It didn't matter to the principal that she was pregnant. She was a student, she had goals, she wanted to go to this school, and she did very well there.

The policy to exclude pregnant students from Karen's school might still be in effect if Cynthia hadn't complained to the school authorities about Karen's expulsion. The next step for Cynthia is to ask to speak to the school's entire staff about Karen's experience. If Cynthia doesn't feel comfortable doing this, perhaps she can find someone else, possibly a pregnancy counselor, to share with the staff the special needs of pregnant students.

If your daughter is attending a private school and you're afraid she'll be expelled because of her pregnancy, talk first with the administrators. You can request that your daughter be honored as an individual, and explain that now is when she needs the most support, rather than when she's in a more positive place in her life.

Change generally happens only when someone advocates for that change. "Rattle some cages. It helps!" advises Marge Eliason, Young Families Program, Billings, Montana.

School for Pregnant Teens

Doris and her daughter Melinda lived in another town during much of Melinda's pregnancy because they agreed Melinda would be better off in the special school for pregnant and parenting teenagers. There were no special services in their home town. Doris talked about the school:

In the school she was very much a minority because she was considering adoption. It was a big school and most of the girls kept their babies. Melinda had friends there, but I think they all wondered why she was different. In so many cases, the girls' mothers had decided they'd keep the babies. You wonder what will happen several years down the road.

There was child care on campus, so Melinda saw the girls coming to school with their babies. She saw what a tough situation it was. I think that actually helped her understand that parenting isn't all fun and games.

Maternity Home for Melissa

Some young women prefer to attend a special school while they're pregnant. Other families choose alternative living arrangements for their daughter during the last few months of her pregnancy.

Toni had never thought about maternity homes until she learned her 15-year-old daughter, Melissa, was pregnant:

Melissa was in her sixth month when she told us. We stayed awake all night talking and crying. Then the next day I turned on the TV, and there was a public service announcement about St. Anne's, a place I'd never heard of before. It's not far from where I work, and I discovered that in California the state pays the fee for a pregnant teenager staying there.

It's a place where the girls are nurtured and not looked down on. More people in this situation should know about places like this.

Melissa decided she wanted to go to St. Anne's. It was strictly her choice because by then she was considering adoption. I made it very clear to her that it was her choice, and that if she decided to keep her baby, I would do everything possible to help her raise it. I also told her I would support adoption – but that doesn't take away the pain.

The baby's father wasn't being supportive, and that was partly why Melissa decided to go to St. Anne's. She was hurting because she was totally dependent on him for support, and she wasn't getting that support.

At first, Melissa was unhappy about considering St. Anne's because she'd never been away from home before. When we visited the home, however, she thought it was nice.

I think she had a problem with homesickness the first night she was there, but Melissa saw it as a solution for the next three months. At that point, she hadn't decided whether to adopt or keep. A lot of the girls at St. Anne's do keep their babies.

I saw her every single day because I work in downtown Los Angeles. When I called Melissa the first day she was there, she fell apart on the phone. I told her I'd come by every day, and I did.

Melissa graduated while she was at St. Anne's. Her diploma came from her own school, but she chose not to go through the graduation ceremony. Not too many people knew she was pregnant, although when she went away, the rumors started.

Is Marriage a Solution?

What about marriage? Years ago, if a man's teenage daughter got pregnant, he expected the man (or boy) who caused the pregnancy to marry her.

The boy's parents may have felt this was the only honorable thing to do, too. Beth, who was devastated when she learned her son, Doug, had caused Roseanne's pregnancy, discussed this issue:

I have always thought that pregnancy is not a good basis
for marriage because I feel so strongly that marriage is a
life-long commitment. I had voiced this to my neighbor,
who later was appalled that adoption was a possibility. I
had told her I really thought adoption was an option.
Choosing a Christian family with the same beliefs makes it
possible.

My first question was, "Are you guys planning to get
married?" That would have been my husband's choice.

Doug said, "I don't know. We've talked about it, but I
don't think that's what we'll do."

Roseanne was 15, mature for her age, but in no way
ready to parent. Doug was 18, and he wasn't emotionally
mature. I felt it would be foolish to push marriage on these
two youngsters.

*The divorce rate for teenagers under 18 who marry because
of pregnancy is four times as high as is the divorce rate for
couples who marry in their 20s. If your daughter or son is
considering marriage because of too-early pregnancy, you
would be wise to encourage extreme caution before making this
big decision.*

Teenage Marriage: Coping with Reality *by Lindsay (Morning Glory Press, 1988) offers a good discussion of early marriage. Young couples, married or living together as teenagers,
share their experiences of coping with little money, living with
his parents or hers, and other difficulties of too-early marriage.*

*Many teenage couples find early marriage a hard, arduous
and sudden transition to an adulthood for which neither is
prepared. If she is already pregnant, the couple's life together
has an even more risky beginning.*

Parents Advise Against Marriage

*Ted and Mary Lou felt strongly that Stacy and Ed were too
young to consider marriage. In fact, when they learned of
Stacy's pregnancy, they told her they didn't want her to see Ed
any more.*

Mary Lou said bluntly, "We don't harbor resentments toward Ed, but he's a boy, he's not a man yet. Suggesting those two children marry at that age was ridiculous. I think they resented us for stopping their relationship at first, but we thought they needed some time to think things out."

"That first day, when Stacy told us she was pregnant," Ted added, "I told her she and Ed could no longer see each other. I didn't think that was appropriate. After a few days, Stacy began to understand my reasoning and she accepted it. Being young, they had a lot of romantic ideas, but realistically, Stacy knew that wouldn't work."

Stacy apparently accepted her parents' request that she not continue to see Ed. For other teenagers, such an approach might create a great deal of resentment toward the parents. Perhaps it worked with Stacy because her parents were extremely supportive of her needs generally, and she already had a great deal of respect for their decisions.

The young woman couldn't tolerate the tug of war between the two families.

Sharon Kaplan, Parenting Resources, described a situation where the above approach backfired. There was no counseling before birth for either birthparent, and the young woman couldn't tolerate the tug of war between the two families. So they ran away and got married.

"We hear a lot of 'You'll never see this person again' when we're talking with pregnant teenagers and their parents," Kaplan commented.

"When you see the young couple together in counseling sessions, they may appear to have a healthy relationship," Kaplan continued. "However, the fact of the pregnancy may be enough to destroy anything good as far as the birthgrandparents are concerned.

"We need to remember that anger is a part of grieving. We like to get both families in our office so we can help them deal with the anger and the grieving.

*"Sometimes young birthmoms need to complete that relation-
ship with the birthfather," Kaplan mused. "I've talked to older
birthmothers who have discussed the need to go back and have a
love relationship with the man who fathered her child. They tell
me they either need to put those feelings to rest or marry him.
Otherwise it's a fantasy."*

If She's Very Young

*A pregnant woman, no matter how young she is, has the legal
right to choose whether she will terminate her pregnancy, keep
her child to rear herself, or have her child, then place him/her
for adoption. This can be difficult for parents to understand,
especially if their pregnant daughter is very young. Diane and
Howard's daughter Kristie was 14 when she had her baby.
Diane shared their frustrations:*

It's a whole different ball game for a 14-year-old
compared to a 17-year-old. It's been incredible, some of
the laws. Basically she has all the rights, yet if she went
next door and damaged someone's house, I'm liable. At
first, that was hard to understand.

The emotional turmoil was tremendous. Kristi's attitude
was not "I'm really sorry. This is a mess, please help me
out." Instead she was real real defensive. It was tough to be
loving and supportive.

We met with a counselor and found out about their
program where families in their church open their homes to
pregnant teenagers. It seemed like a good idea, especially
since Kristi didn't seem to want to stay in our neighbor-
hood. We figured she needed to get out of here.

Part of it is her sister. Pati's 13, and she and Kristi are
very different people. At one point while Kristi was still at
home, Pati was screaming at her. It started out with a
typical sisterly argument. Kristi called Pati stupid, and Pati
said, "I'm not stupid. I'm not the one that went out and had
sex and got pregnant."

Pati went with us when we met the family where Kristi
stayed until her baby was born. That family is incredible.

They have seven kids including a 14-year-old daughter.

They're much more strict than we are. Kristi always thought it was weird that we wanted to know where she was, and now she sees that maybe we were fair after all. That's been good.

While Kristi was there, the family provided temporary shelter for a battered wife with a couple of kids. The young woman told Kristi how horrible we were to make Kristi give the baby up. She told Kristi she could keep the baby and go to Colorado to live with her.

Kristi got angry and said, "These (adoptive couple) are good parents. I don't want my baby to be on welfare." So even though it was hard on her and really upset her, it was a good encounter.

We visit Kristi every couple of weeks. My mom writes to Kristi and sends her little gifts.

Two months after the above conversation, Kristi delivered a little boy. His adoptive parents took him home from the hospital the day Kristi returned to her family.

Parents Need Help Too

Claire Priester, House of Ruth Ministries, Downey, California, talked about her work with young people and with their parents. "I try to provide emotional support for my clients' parents because so often they feel they've been failures as parents," she said. "Their first reaction may be, 'How will this affect me? How could you do this to me?' Well, their parents weren't even in their minds when this happened.

"Next the parents wonder how this will affect their child, and they realize she (or he) needs their support.

"I find a lot of parents feeling they need to punish their child. They'll put her on restriction, not let her do any fun things. 'We want her to experience the consequences,' they'll say, 'We want her to be responsible for what she's done.' They start putting these heavy burdens on her.

"I tell them there are plenty of heavy decisions here. They can support their teenager best by working through their own

*emotions as best they can. They need to see how much of what
they're experiencing is really just emotional stuff, then try to
back away from that and help their daughter make a decision*

*When too-early pregnancy happens, parents need to deal with
their own feelings. At the same time, they face the responsibility
of helping their teenager cope as well as possible with the
months ahead.*

Tom, Roseanne's father, expressed his feelings succinctly:

First I was mad. I had no idea anything was wrong.
After I got over the initial shock, all I could think about
was, "She's my girl. Forget about being mad. Let's help
each other."

We had no desire to hurt anyone, either Roseanne or
Doug, and we let them know they had our support. We had
things to do, and we'd better get with it.

3

WHAT ABOUT
THE BIRTHFATHER?

Teenage single fathers vary a great deal. They represent all ethnic and socio-economic groups, and their education varies from almost none to those with college credit. Many still live with their parents while others are on their own. Some are very involved with their children while others are not.

Teenage mothers also come from all socio-economic and ethnic groups. Some live at home and receive a great deal of support from their parents. Others are kicked out because of pregnancy.

These young mothers, however, unlike some fathers, have one thing in common. They bond with their babies during pregnancy. They love their babies. Those who consider adoption love their babies just as parents do who rear their children themselves. I have never known or heard of a birthmother who didn't love her child, and who would not have liked to parent him/her. For her, adoption is a difficult and loving option.

Generalizing about birthfathers is harder.

The Birthfather's Role

Some young birthfathers are responsible young men who want and need to be involved in planning for this baby. Theoretically, both parents should have the right to make and carry out an adoption plan for their baby, or plan to keep the baby to rear together or for either one to rear alone.

The birthfather's signature is needed in most states for an adoption to become final. If he doesn't want the adoption to occur, legally he generally has a right to prevent it.

While a small percentage of married couples make and carry out an adoption plan for their child, most adoptions are planned because the baby's parents are not married. They aren't likely even to have a close relationship.

In some cases the father has vanished. In others, he says, "That's not my baby." Other young men feel impregnating a woman signifies manhood. Teenagers tell stories of the young man who fathers several babies but feels responsible for none.

A teacher of a school program for pregnant teenagers reports having two students one year who were pregnant by the same 18-year-old football player. One was 17, a high school senior planning to go to college. She was considering an adoption plan. The other student was 14, and planned to keep her baby. She and her family relied on welfare for financial support.

The young father, who never showed up for any counseling sessions, was determined his baby would not be "given away." If the 17-year-old didn't want her child, he wanted his 14-year-old girlfriend to keep and care not only for her own baby, but also for his other child.

Because of this possibility, the 17-year-old mother decided to keep her child even though it meant sacrificing her goals for herself and her goal that her child be reared by two parents.

Most of the interviews for this book were with birthmothers' families. Judging from the majority of these interviews, the birthfather caused a tremendous amount of pain. The pregnancy may not be seen solely as his "fault," but he was the bad guy in several of the adoption-planning accounts. Sometimes neither he nor his family was consulted concerning the proposed adoption. It was assumed that he wouldn't care.

Negative Feelings Toward Birthfather

Cynthia still has extremely bitter feelings toward daughter Karen's boyfriend, John:

We don't care for the father at all. We've had a lot of problems with him. I would never ever want him to parent Karen's baby. I'd have done almost anything to keep that from happening.

John is a high school dropout who is involved in drugs and alcohol. I've seen him do unsafe things with a baby. No way can we let that happen.

Karen told John he could visit her in the hospital, and he came in with his mother and his sister. They almost wrecked the whole adoption plan. None of them were prepared for the emotions they experienced when they saw the baby.

Everything boils down to this very short span of time, and you don't know if you'll get through it. He was there, and all of a sudden he had to deal with it. "This is my baby. You aren't going to take my baby away from me," he was saying. We didn't want him there trying to influence Karen.

I called Dorothy, Karen's counselor, and she came over. We understood that John as the father had rights, but this was a sudden totally unplanned development. He had agreed two weeks earlier to sign the adoption papers.

John said to the counselor, "You know it's Karen's parents who are making her do this."

"Is that true, Karen?" Dorothy asked.

"No, it isn't. I know I'm not ready to parent," Karen replied.

The three of them talked for at least 30 minutes, and John agreed that adoption was best for his son.

I'm glad Dorothy was there. I don't think we could have handled it alone.

Dorothy, Karen's counselor, commented:

Karen had an easier time dealing with the release than she did with the relationship.

John walked into Karen's labor room, kissed her, and said, "We can do it." His mother came into her room and said she'd help them with the baby.

I had gone home to get some rest after Scott was born. Karen called me almost immediately, saying, "Please, get back here."

---

*Those were the hardest four days
of Karen's life.*

John's mother came in and looked me straight in the eyes, saying, "We have two mature adults here making this decision."

I felt like saying, "You have a 15-year-old here who has just had a baby, and your son wasn't around at all during the pregnancy."

I didn't say a word, but Karen said, "That's not true. I'm only 15 years old."

John said to me, "It's her mother who's making her give up the baby."

That's the one time I stepped over the boundaries of counseling. I said, "She knows that's not the way it is."

He looked at Karen and said, "Is that true?"

"Yes," she replied.

I think Karen wavered in her decision because the flowers came, John was there. But when push came to shove. . .

Her parents were scared to death. Those were the hardest four days of Karen's life, but she had made her decision a long time ago, at seven months. Most birthmothers do. At that time, they want to pick a family, and their whole focus changes. They're ready. They've made up their minds, and they call me to say, "Tell them I've chosen them. They have to get ready for the baby."

If the father is not with the mother during pregnancy, he's likely to be in a different place emotionally than the mother. Obviously Karen was with her baby every minute from the time she conceived until delivery. She bonded with the baby during pregnancy, while John wasn't there during this important time. "Should" John have been more involved with the adoption decision? It's a difficult question.

Birthfather's Parents Fight Adoption

Lilia's mother, Georgia, was furious with Darrell, 17. Lilia and Darrell were not allowed to date, only to spend time together at each other's homes. They broke up in December, and Lilia didn't tell her parents she was pregnant until two months later. Two weeks before Tiara was born, Georgia related:

One of my biggest problems is forgiving Darrell. I can't get over this hump. We had trusted him, and we didn't want him around any more. I didn't want to hear his voice, didn't want to see his face, didn't want to see him on our street.

Actually, he's concerned for Lilia and for the baby. He acknowledged it was his baby, but of course he isn't taking responsibility – he's only 17.

Lilia went through a period of romanticism because she was having a baby. It made my blood boil. This is romantic – two children having a baby?

Darrell's parents didn't call or come see us. I resented that. If my son did that, I'd immediately ask what we could do. A month or two after Lilia told us, I mustered up strength to go see them. We talked about adoption and Darrell said, "No way, not my baby." His parents didn't like the idea, and they said they could keep the baby.

That's not a solution – that's such a cruel thing to say. People don't realize what adoption is all about, that it's a caring, loving thing.

Darrell said he'd get a job, and his father said he'd see that Darrell would support the baby. That was Darrell's solution – to keep the baby himself. I said, "What would you do with it?"

"I can love it," he said.

I was shocked when his parents said, "Give it to us."

As we left, we said adoption was what we wanted, and that Darrell and Lilia shouldn't see each other any more.

"I want you to keep the baby, and I will love it."

I wrote Darrell a letter a month ago because I didn't think he knew what "Sorry" meant. I didn't think he knew how much this has broken up our family. I wanted him to understand what we were going through, what Lilia was going through, and how hard the months ahead were going to be.

One instant had changed our lives. I told him I wasn't able to forgive him then, but I was trying.

Even now I don't think he understands. He said he understood why she was making an adoption plan, but did he *really* understand?

His general attitude was, "I want you to keep the baby, and I will love it." In other words, he wouldn't give up anything, but he'd have the benefit of seeing his baby grow. He'd be able to say, "That's my baby." A very prideful thing.

Lilia has talked to Darrell about the adoption. He wants to be there when the baby is born, but I said, "Absolutely not! He's not your husband. Just because he fathered the baby doesn't mean he should be there."

He has refused to talk to the adoption counselor.

A couple of days ago, with the baby due in two weeks, Darrell's father called Lilia and said, "We'd like to throw a baby shower for you."

"What would I need a baby shower for?" she asked. "I'm giving the baby up for adoption."

"You don't want to do that," he said. "You want to think about it. You'll live to regret this."

Lilia is a pretty strong kid, but this made her feel bad. She said, "No, thank you, I don't want a baby shower."

"Well, let us know when you're ready, and we'll do it," he said, as if he hadn't heard her at all.

I was so upset at the baby shower call that I decided to
write Darrell's parents a letter. I didn't want to hurt them
by saying unkind things. But these people don't stop to
realize what they're doing, that they're tearing down what
it has taken us months to accomplish. Then for them to call
and say, "You're going to regret this." Of course she's
going to regret this!

This is the letter I sent them. I think it helped because
they quit calling Lilia.

"Dear Frank and Denise,

I want to thank you for your concern regarding Lilia's
and Darrell's baby, and thank you for letting us come over
to talk.

Lilia is doing well and has found a wonderful, loving
Christian couple for the baby. She is happy and excited for
them, that she can give them such a great gift. She is happy
that she can fill this mother's longing, empty arms.

We have prayed and continue to pray about this daily. I
now realize that God is in control here, that He has sent
these parents for the baby, and that God has given Lilia the
strength and peace we have been requesting for so long.
And we know that "all things work together for good to
those who love God." (Romans 8:28)

*Please respect our household
and our decisions made in it.*

When your daughter became pregnant the first time, you
said you wanted to throw her out. Instead, you chose to let
her make her own decision. You stood by her and you
supported her in it.

Again your daughter hurt you and became pregnant.
Again you have decided to stand by and support her in it.
Will she someday live to "regret" what she has done?
Maybe so, and maybe not, only God knows.

We also have let Lilia make her own decision, and we
also will stand by her and support her in it. She too may

live to regret her decision, but she'll handle that when and if the time comes.

Please respect our household and our decisions made in it. We again thank you for your concern, but a decision has been made, and we are working as a family toward it.

We anticipate Lilia will go through an emotional time in the hospital, and we want to allow her that time with peace. For this reason, we do not want many visitors in the hospital. We are only going to allow Lilia's other dad and Darrell to be there. We again ask for your respect in this family decision. We will honor our promise to send you pictures as we receive them.

Thank you for your time, understanding and cooperation in this matter. I pray that you will someday have God's peace in this.

Sincerely,

Georgia

Before she delivered, Lilia commented:

At first Darrell would say, "Oh, you don't love it, you want to give it away." At first I treated him mean because he wouldn't say what I wanted to hear. We didn't talk for awhile.

When my mom and dad met with his parents and talked about adoption, they said, "Oh, we'll keep it." A three-bedroom house with nine people in it? I don't want my baby to live like that.

When I was choosing the parents, I didn't talk with Darrell's parents. I probably should have so they would know I was still planning to do this. Finally, I wrote Darrell a letter and explained everything. It floored him. He had assumed I wasn't doing anything about it, that I wouldn't do it. He was shocked. He told me the other day that he reads the letter a lot.

I talked to him a couple of days ago, and he said, "Yes, I'll support you. It might be the right thing to do." Then he added, "I just don't want you to regret it later."

I said, "I regret other things, a lot of things, but this is best for the baby."

"I don't know how you can be so happy about this whole thing," he said. That's because he hasn't gone through everything, talking with Amy (my counselor), choosing the parents, getting to know them.

But he's willing to go along with it. He'll sign the papers.

Lilia Copes with Her Grieving

Two weeks later Lilia delivered a little girl. She described her labor and birth experience, then talked about the adoption:

We called Maggie and Al, the adoptive parents, when I was in labor, and they came to the hospital. Maggie was in the delivery room along with my mother. My dad and Darrell were right outside the door, and they heard the baby's first cry.

Darrell's parents kept calling me two or three weeks before Tiara was born to say, "Why are you doing this?" They really got to me and I told my mom to change our phone number. That's when she called them and wrote the letter. We didn't want to go through that at the hospital. They never bothered us after Tiara was born.

Maggie called me yesterday and said her church had a baby shower for her, and 85 women were there. The whole church had been praying for Maggie because they knew how much she hurt because she couldn't have a baby. She said she had nearly 200 gifts – she couldn't believe it. "This little girl is looking like she came out of *Vogue* magazine," she said.

I'm fine now. The first week was the hardest. I wasn't only down, but when I was down, I was *down*. After that I felt stronger every day.

The first time Maggie called me, it hurt to hear her say good things about Tiara. I felt jealous. I was crying inside, but I didn't want her to know. I hung up, and I was depressed because I missed the baby.

Maggie said she'd call me in a couple of days. To me that was two days, and I was counting down. To her it meant several days or a week.

So two days went by and she didn't call, and I was so down. Then the third day I got some pictures from her and a letter, including a really pretty big close-up picture of Tiara. She is so cute. I felt a little better, but I still wanted to hear Maggie's voice. I wanted her to call me.

I called Amy and she said she'd come over to see me. "What do you want from Maggie?" she asked.

I said I'd like Maggie to call me at least once a week for awhile. I wanted pictures, and I wanted to get a gift and take it over to Tiara. I wanted to see her one more time.

I said, "I don't know whether this is asking too much – I've never done this before." Amy thought this would be OK.

Maggie called me, and I said, "Oh, you must have talked to Amy." She hadn't. Maggie did it on her own, and that pleased me. She told me all these things about Tiara, how she kind of snorts when she wants to eat because she's so hungry. She lifts her head, and she's only ten days old!

My feelings now are like all that hurt turned into happiness for Tiara. I did this because I want more for my baby. I did it for her, so I don't hurt a lot.

Darrell is fine. He went to the hospital, and he fell in love with Maggie and Al. He hugged them and said later, "I like them a lot. She's so pretty." Everything went well.

It's right, the way it should be.
I'll get over my hurt
and everything will be fine.

They're going to let me see her again. Darrell wants to go with me, but I said, "No, that's not fair. At the beginning, you didn't want me to place her for adoption. You were totally against it. You didn't go with me to pick them out, to meet them, to get to know them, to find out what kind of people they are. And now you expect to go visit them, and you want their address, their phone number, that's not fair."

Maybe if he'd been there in the beginning, maybe it would have been all right, but not now. I told him, "You only met them one time one day, and that was that. If you want to get Tiara a gift, that's fine. Give it to me and I'll take it to her."

The only bad thing about this is that I hurt. Everything else came out good. It's right, the way it should be. I'll get over my hurt and everything will be fine.

Amy said it was like a death in the family except there's no grave. You go through a period of sadness and depression, but then you start to feel better. It still hurts, but you can go on with your life. And that's how it is really, just getting over it, the fact that she's not here any more. You live with it.

Native American Adoption Law

Luke's planned adoption was in danger. When his birthfather went to the adoption agency office to sign the adoption papers, he mentioned he was part Native American. There are special laws pertaining to the adoption of Native American children. These laws supercede state and federal adoption laws.

Luke had been with his adoptive parents several months when this happened. His father's announcement temporarily put a stop to the legal proceedings, to the consternation of the adoptive parents and to Luke's birthmother, Becky.

A few months later, the legal problems were worked out, and the adoption became final.

If you're involved in an adoption plan for a baby with a birthparent of Native American heritage, no matter how slight, check the laws carefully before you proceed with the plan.

Phil Supports Adoption

Sometimes the birthfather is appalled at this pregnancy. Both he and his parents may feel adoption is the only rational, loving approach. Phil, 23, described his strong feelings:

It was one of the few times in my life when all of a
sudden everything seemed to go wrong. I learned of this
pregnancy when I went over to Leesa's apartment intend-
ing to break up with her. She was 19, we had been dating
for six months, and I knew our relationship wasn't
working.

Leesa had learned that day that she was pregnant. I
couldn't ignore it, but we did break up. In fact, the whole
pregnancy was a long drawn out break-up. I had finally
decided to straighten out my life, and that our relationship
wasn't right for either of us. When I learned she was
pregnant, all my good intentions seemed for nothing. That
was hard.

> *Raising the child didn't make any sense*
> *for any of us, me, Leesa, or the baby.*

We looked at all the options. Raising the child didn't
make any sense to me for any of us, me, Leesa, or the
baby. I'm real big on the whole family situation which is
the way I've grown up.

Leesa grew up very differently. Her perspective through
the whole pregnancy was mostly that single parenting is
OK. Everyone does it now, and supposedly there is no
damage to the child. I didn't want my child to grow up that
way. Even if I were to raise it, I knew I couldn't provide a
complete family.

I told my parents a month or so later. For the first week I
think it put a real strain on their relationship with each
other as they tried to talk about it.

A couple of months later Leesa saw a lawyer because
she had a friend who wanted a baby. I wasn't impressed
with this couple, and I didn't want to go that route. Someone suggested I call Christian Adoption and Family
Services. I did, and I was impressed with their counseling
and their caring.

I was the one who mostly fought for adoption. I felt I
was arguing for that child. Leesa thought she was doing the

same. The relationship Leesa and I had was not good, yet she was fighting for that relationship. It seemed to me that the child became a pawn as we argued. She would say, "Maybe I should never have told you." "Maybe I should have had an abortion." "Maybe I should keep the child." Our focus was not the same.

We started seeing Angela at the agency in May, and we returned every two or three weeks, sometimes together and sometimes separately, but usually alone. Leesa went back and forth about adoption.

The hardest time was after Lucy was born. Because she had a C-section, Leesa was in the hospital for four days which meant we got to see the baby those days. That was my only time with Lucy, and I wanted to make the most of it. I had made my decision, and I didn't regret it. Lucy would be gone soon, but I wanted those four days with her.

I argued for the adoption.
Leesa argued for us to be together.

Leesa had mixed feelings. She knew how I felt, but she had a hard time accepting adoption. Every night after the baby was taken back to the nursery, we argued. I argued for the adoption, and Leesa argued for us to be together. The baby didn't seem to be the real issue with Leesa.

The last night I had had enough arguing. I knew this was the last night and that the next morning would be the last time I'd see Lucy. At that point I started crying. I was tired of arguing, and this was my heartache too.

This was something Leesa hadn't seen, perhaps because my decision was so clearly made. She thought I had been cold about it, although I didn't think so. At any rate, she was quite affected by seeing how broken up I was. She finally was convinced that I wasn't throwing the baby away as some of her friends had suggested.

The next morning we had a dedication ceremony, and I gave Lucy to the adoptive parents. Leesa didn't go. She didn't think she could handle it. I respected her wishes, but

at the same time I think being there might have helped her
deal with the adoption a little better.

I saw Leesa several times during the first two weeks.
We both went through feeling like we'd died, or we wanted
to. The first month was really tough. Actually it was hard
for four or five months, but after awhile the normal healing
process occurred. We were grieving and we were admitting
our loss, and that helps the process along.

We've talked very briefly three or four times in the year
since Lucy was born.

Phil's Mother Shares Feelings

*Beth, Phil's mother, talked about the pain she and her family
experienced for themselves, for Phil, and for Leesa:*

Our pain was as great as anyone's could be. Perhaps in
some families unmarried pregnancy is more accepted. My
husband is a pastor, and he was devastated. He still is.
Because of his upbringing, it's very hard for him to accept
either the pregnancy or the adoption.

In my family my mother is very accepting. She says,
"Everybody gets in trouble. We'll accept it and go on."

We wanted adoption from the beginning because we felt
it was better for everybody, for Phil, for Leesa, and for the
baby. I have to be honest and say we were protecting
ourselves too.

First of all, we knew Phil didn't love Leesa. He didn't
want to marry her. Marriage wasn't going to solve anything. We felt it would be a millstone around Phil's neck
for the rest of his life if Leesa kept the baby.

Leesa went back and forth on the adoption issue. I went
to see her and took her out to eat right from the beginning
because she had no family here except an aunt. It was very
difficult.

Leesa said, "Why should my child have an unhappy
mother?" But right up to the last minute, nobody was sure
she would go through with the adoption.

She lived in a tiny apartment that she could barely afford and had only a temporary job. Who was going to take care of this child?

We didn't know Leesa well, but we knew she was not the kind of person for Phil.

I knew the adoption decision had to be theirs, and I knew I had to be supportive of Phil too. Right at the end, the last day, he cried. We knew at the time of birth it's very emotional. Friends told us Leesa would try to convince him at the last minute, "I love the baby, you love her. Why don't we get married and raise her together?"

I was proud of Phil. He stuck by his guns and said, "Leesa, we have to do what's best for the baby."

Birthfather Tries to Stop Adoption

Russ learned that his daughter, Mindy, was pregnant when he took her to the hospital to check out her stomach pains. He returned home that evening to prepare supper for his invalid wife. Lee, Mindy's boyfriend, had already heard from Mindy by phone from the hospital, so he came over to talk to Russ.

Russ: When I came home, Lee came over and we talked and we talked. While I was fixing dinner I had a long sharp knife in my hand, and I noticed Lee stayed at the other end of the kitchen. I wasn't feeling friendly.

Lee was talking about wanting to marry Mindy sometime but not right now. I was thinking, "You've had your say, and you can leave any time." He stayed, and he went back to the hospital with me.

About two weeks later his parents invited us over for dinner. We had never met them. We had a good talk although I don't remember them mentioning sharing expenses.

Not long after that Lee and Karen broke up, and two months later Lee was hospitalized because of his problems with drugs. When he came home, he and Mindy talked several times about the adoption plan she was working out. He either wanted her to keep the baby or he wanted it.

Lee Agrees to Sign

*Neither plan seemed wise either to Mindy or to her father.
Lee said he might take legal action if they went ahead with the
adoption. However, soon after the baby was born, he told Mindy
he'd sign the adoption papers. Mindy commented:*

I think my main problem through this was Lee. I tried
not to hurt him but still do what I thought was best for the
baby. Ultimately I had to hurt someone, and that someone
was Lee. I didn't like that, but we're pretty good friends
again now. I can tell his pain is starting to ease some.

Lee's family used to love me, but now they hate me
because I gave Jessica up. They feel like I stole something
from them, and they are real hurt about it.

I went through with it because I kept going back to
thinking what would be best for Jessica. A week before I
had her I decided to change my mind. I talked it over with
my dad, and I talked to the adoptive father for a couple of
hours. He said of course they would be hurt if I changed
my mind, but that that couldn't be helped. He knew I had
to hurt someone. That took some of the pressure off me.

Lee had threatened legal action if we tried to go through
with the adoption, but a week after Jessica was born, he
called me. He said, "I'm not going to try to fight it. I wish
it didn't have to happen to us, but I'll let you make the
decision."

He's signed the papers, and he wants to have some
contact with Jessica. Her adoptive parents have agreed that
will be okay.

*Teenagers who see family in terms of the traditional mother
home with the baby and the father supporting the family may
need some help in understanding their realities. Some 16-year-
olds may be capable of nurturing a baby just as 16-year-olds did
a century ago when teenage marriages were quite common. A
16-year-old father, however, generally has no way in our society
today of supporting his family financially. Adolescents may find
this hard to acknowledge.*

Forgiveness Is Difficult

Yvonne's parents, who were heartbroken because of Yvonne's pregnancy, harbored a great deal of resentment toward her boyfriend, Brian.

Donna spoke of the anger she felt for several months after she learned of her daughter's pregnancy. She also talked about the resolution of these feelings:

We had told Brian he couldn't see Yvonne any more. I had intense feelings about this situation. We were suffering so much, yet he didn't have to make any of the arrangements. He seemed to be getting away with no problems.

One day Brian called and asked if he could come by. Up to that time, I knew I couldn't stand to be in the same room with him. I told him I was by myself, but he could come over. As I turned from the phone, I realized my hateful feelings were leaving. I could talk to him.

Brian came into the house, and we sat down in the living room. He looked down. My first instinct was to say something to try to draw him out, but I thought, "No, this was your idea, I'll let you carry the ball." After an eternity (three or four minutes), he said, "I just wanted to tell you I'm sorry."

I told him how I had felt. I confessed I would have liked to make him suffer. I feel he was sincerely remorseful. He was here for 30 minutes.

"Brian, I hope the best for you, but I want you to know that in no way are you to have any contact with Yvonne," I told him.

> *Here is a man with a child some place else, and it has to hurt terribly.*

His family goes to our church, so we see each other. It's not a strained relationship.

The other night my husband and I went to church, and I saw Brian sitting in his car. As we went by, I wanted to hug him. Here is a man with a child someplace else, and it has to hurt terribly. As we walked by his car, I reached in and hugged him.

Brian's Mother Comments

Brian's mother said:

Most people don't think of the birthfather too much. Or they think of him as a reprobate, this hideous person. But there are two sides to this story. In our society there's a lot of pressure put on boys. Brian was actively pursued by nearly every girl he ever dated. They would pursue him until they caught him.

I had never even thought of the boy's parents before, but we're as much grandparents in this situation as Roseanne's parents are. We're hurting, too, although time does help.

"Birthfathers tend to be damned if they do and damned if they don't," commented Marge Eliason, Young Families Program, Billings, Montana. "If he's supportive, it usually means he'll have to be an active parent which almost surely means he'll have to drop out of school. Often, the love affair has died down by this time, he may not like the mom any more, and she can't stand him.

"If he's not supportive," Eliason continued, "he's a terrible person. If he wants to release the baby for adoption and she doesn't, he has no rights. If she wants to release the baby and he doesn't, he's an even more terrible person. It's a no-win situation."

Eliason also talked about the mixed messages the young man is likely to get: "You must be responsible." "She's a tramp – you don't owe her anything. It's probably not your baby." And "But if it is your baby, by God, you have rights, son, and you get in there and fight for them."

"People see the young man as that macho stud," John Holzhuter, Catholic Social Service, Topeka, Kansas, commented. "I've dealt with hundreds of young men, and almost always during the first or second session, their fear, their anger,

and their sadness comes out. Time after time they say, 'I just don't know what to do. I'm not old enough to be a father.'

"I look at these handsome young men and I see their fear, I hear it." Holzhuter encourages his clients to talk with him about their expectations for their own fathers as well as what they want for their own children.

"I try to figure out what their pain and their fears and their anger are, and then try to help them with it. I try to speak to their fear, their aspirations, their humiliation, their pain. I try to get them to explore what they have to offer to the baby and to the mother. They need a chance to communicate what they're thinking," he explained.

Holzhuter also talked about his work with birthgrandparents. He explained, "I have to realize it's not my business to get invested in what happens here. There are two sets of grandparents and two parents. I find it's helpful to get the two families in here together, then help them process their feelings, their desires in the situation. I've seen some unexpected turnabouts between the two sets of parents."

Reuben Pannor, author of **The Unmarried Father** *(Springer, 1971) strongly recommends including the birthfather in the pregnancy counseling. If the birthfather is involved in the counseling process, both he and the birthmother can seriously explore their possible alternatives, and are more likely to agree on the important adoption vs. keeping decision.*

When this happens, the birthfather isn't left feeling guilty, that he didn't do the "right" thing.

If the adoptive parents know that the birthfather was involved in making the adoption plan and some of his reasons for doing so, they can share this with the child as s/he grows older. It's not good for the child to think his/her birthfather didn't care.

Jason's Mother Opposes Adoption

Adoption was unheard of in Celina's large family, and she never approved of Jason allowing his baby to be adopted. She was concerned because Jason never received any counseling whatsoever regarding the adoption decision. Celina talked about the situation:

I came from a big family – ten kids, and adoption in our family was never heard of. I don't know anybody in my family who ever adopted out a child. I can't even think of anyone being adopted into the family.

We had lived here only a few months. Jason has always been a popular boy, and he started seeing Danielle all the time. I kept after him that he was seeing her way too much. He was 17, she was 16, and she had a car. We live out of town, and she'd drive out here every morning to pick him up to go to school.

One day Danielle's mother called. "Is Danielle there?"

"No."

"Is Jason there?"

"No."

She told me her older daughter had come home for lunch and found Danielle packing. Her mother said, "You know she's pregnant, don't you?"

I told her I had no idea. Then she vented her feelings for awhile. I explained that I had been concerned that they were seeing too much of each other. I said it was certainly Jason's problem as much as Danielle's, but he wasn't going to take all the blame.

She found Danielle at the home of one of Jason's friends, and brought her back home.

I asked Jason what they were going to do. "She's talking adoption," he said. That really knocked the wind out of me. I went out to hang up clothes and I cried and I cried.

> *I felt she was getting a lot*
> *of pressure from her mother.*

Danielle moved down to St. Anne's Maternity Home, and Jason and I went to see her several times. Every time we saw her, I'd ask Danielle if she really wanted to adopt that baby out. I felt she was getting a lot of pressure from her mother. She told me one day that she would like to keep her baby, but she felt she was too young. Her folks were approaching retirement age and couldn't help her. I told her I would do what I could if she wanted to keep the baby, but I didn't tell her that's what she ought to do.

Danielle's mother was having a fit because Jason wasn't working. He'd just finished high school, but her mother was saying he was a bum, that Danielle should adopt the baby out and forget him.

Danielle called Jason and told him to get a job. He thought he could get work in another town, so he left a week before the baby was born.

---

*Right up to the last minute I was hoping
the adoption wouldn't happen.*

Danielle was trying to reach him after she delivered, but the two of them never got together to talk while she was in the hospital. I know she wanted to wait and get Jason's final word to go ahead and release the baby.

Danielle had picked out Pete and Belinda to be the adoptive parents, and we met them. The adoption counselor asked Danielle whose idea it was to release the baby for adoption. She said it was Jason's. Jason told me later this wasn't true, but I don't know. . .

Right up to the last minute I was hoping the adoption wouldn't happen, but it did. Jason and Danielle split up soon after the baby was born.

Jason never talked about the adoption. Danielle told me Jason had said, "How could we take care of a little baby when neither of us can take care of ourselves?" I'm a single parent, and he knows how hard it is for me to take care of the family I have. He didn't see how I could be much help.

Danielle received a lot of counseling, and I think that helped her deal with the baby going. Jason had none. He had to keep his feelings to himself, and I know there was a lot bothering him.

We'd go to department stores, and he'd pick up little dresses, look at them, then put them back down. I don't

know what went through his mind because he never said
anything.

If Jason had had the counseling that Danielle had, it
could have had a good effect. She seemed pretty balanced
about it all. I asked her once how she was doing, and she
said it wasn't too bad because she thought of the baby as
her niece.

*Sharon Kaplan, Parenting Resources, feels the biggest block
to getting counseling for the father is the young birthmother who
doesn't want him involved. "If I'm seeing her," Kaplan explained, "we assign the paternal family to another staff
member."*

*Recently more birthfathers and their families are involved in
adoption planning, according to Kaplan. She suggests this may
be because of her organization's emphasis on benefits to the
child in a well-planned adoption.*

*"I can't believe the feelings of the paternal grandparents are
all that different from those of the maternal grandparents. This
boy's family has feelings, too," Kaplan concluded.*

4

CONSIDERING
AN ADOPTION PLAN

*Many pregnant teenagers and their families never consider
an adoption plan for their babies. Those who don't choose
abortion feel that, because they are pregnant, they **must** become
acting parents, whether single or married. They don't believe
they have choices either for themselves or for their children.*

*The teenager's parents may also believe strongly that if a
baby is born into the family, the baby **must** be reared in
that family.*

*Deanne's parents were shocked to learn they would be grand-
parents in three months. They have six children, three younger
than Deanne, and their first impression was that of course they
would keep the baby and raise it as their own. Within a week,
however, Deanne's mother, Thila, started wondering about
the baby. . .*

There was something in my head that said there is
someone involved here who can't speak for him/herself.
We weren't even considering adoption. . .but maybe this

unborn person deserved more than being raised as our grandchild/child with a child-mother. I contacted a counselor at Catholic Social Service and took Deanne to visit her. Deanne continued to see her until the baby was born and for several months afterward.

My husband and I saw a different counselor at Catholic Social Service. We saw him weekly both before and after the baby was born. In fact, we continued to see him occasionally for several years. We'd touch base with him at least once a year.

> *Maybe this unborn person deserved more than being raised as our grandchild/child with a child-mother.*

In the beginning Deanne felt adoption was not an option. At first I think she felt we were trying to steal the baby and control her, but I feel sure she made the final decision.

We never met the adoptive parents Deanne selected. Deanne brought home the letters describing the families, and we read them too. After reading one, all I could do was cry.

"What do you think, Mom?" Deanne asked.

"It's not my decision, but they're the ones I'd pick," I replied.

"I've already chosen them," she said.

Deanne even sent home with the baby a bouquet of flowers she'd received in the hospital. She wanted him to have them.

It's very hard, but you muddle through the best you possibly can.

Parental Guidance Is Needed

Marge Driscoll, Holy Family Services, Los Angeles, recommends that parents listen to their kids. "They've got to stop being judgmental and try to understand what's going on with their daughter. That's hard when they're so angry at the young woman," she points out.

"The other thing I think kids need – although they would never admit this – is some guidance from their parents," Driscoll continues. "They need to be able to talk about the options, adoption and keeping, but they also have to know where the bottom line is. Many parents can't do this.

*"Some parents appear to be so enmeshed in the situation that they think they can be a parent to the teenager **and** to the baby. They have a hard time talking about the hopes and dreams they have for their daughter, and how important they think it is for that daughter to consider those hopes and dreams as she makes her decision.*

"If the parents really feel this child should come into their family, that they can provide a good lifestyle, and that this would be good for their daughter, then they need to let her know that.

"Often they don't say this. There is always a message, but when it's not stated clearly, the kids may decide to wait until the baby is born to make a decision. Yet no person is ever more vulnerable than a woman after she has given birth. That is not the time to make the decision between adoption and keeping," Driscoll stresses.

Helping Her See Reality

When Kristi became pregnant at 14, she and her boyfriend, 18, planned to keep their baby and have a wonderful life together. Kristi's mother, Diane, explained in chapter 2 why Kristi moved in with another family during her pregnancy. Diane continues their story:

Kristi is basically a good kid, but last year was a bad time for her. However, the growth and maturing we see now is amazing.

We visit her often, and she looks forward to seeing us. She realizes now that an adoption plan is best.

We have all met the adoptive couple Kristi selected, and she's gone to lunch with them. We're excited for them.

You know, as a mother, you're always protective of your own. I find it amazing to see the number of emotions we go through. First and foremost, I'm out to protect my child. And that's really special for Kristi to see, that we'll always be there no matter how tough it gets.

In the beginning she was rebelling. No matter what we said, she'd do the opposite. She and her boyfriend were going to keep the child.

When we first visited the adoption counselor, Kristi was asked why she was considering adoption. "Because they're making me," she said as she pointed at us. Of course the counselor commented gently that this was not reason enough, that it had to be Kristi's decision.

We told her we weren't trying to force adoption.

We have several friends who have adopted children. One morning my husband took Kristi to visit three of these families. "This is what these people can do for their children," he said.

Then he took Kristi on a tour of the not-so-good parts of town. "This is probably your other choice because you'd have to be on welfare," he told her. That's about the time she apparently started thinking in terms of what's good for the baby.

We told her we weren't trying to force adoption. We also told her we weren't willing to parent another child. If she kept her baby, she could live with us for three years, but she would have the complete responsibility for her child's care.

Our high school has a small daycare center for students' babies, so Kristi knew it would have been possible. That was important – that she not continue to think we made her place her child for adoption.

As far as I can tell, she feels real good about it now. She feels she herself is still a child. We told her we aren't ready to give her up yet.

As the grandparent – that's a hard term for me – I feel great about the adoption. This couple is super, and Kristi's child will have the best start any family could give it. We think adoptive families are real special people.

Birthgrandparents Need Help

Bonnie Adkins-DeJong, and Jean Kennedy, Bethany Christian Services, Bellflower, California, work with many of the parents of their birthparent clients.

"Grandparents sometimes have a more difficult time than birthparents. We're running into that phenomenon more and more," commented Adkins-DeJong. "The younger the girl, the harder it is for grandparents, perhaps because they believe they're capable of parenting that child."

"Recently a birthgrandparent was in here in tears. She told me, 'I'm 34 years old and I'm encouraging my daughter to make an adoption plan. Yet the adoptive couple you're placing her baby with are older than I am,'" Kennedy related. "She was experiencing guilt because she thought she should rear her daughter's child, and she didn't want to start over after caring for three children of her own."

"I've also seen birthgrandmothers adamantly opposing their daughter's decision to carry out an adoption plan," continued Adkins-DeJong. "They say, 'You're giving away my flesh and blood!' Usually the birthmom is older, perhaps college age, if she releases without parental support. Very young birthmoms have a tough time considering adoption if Mom and Dad aren't interested."

Kennedy described a situation where a birthgrandmother said to her daughter, who was still in the hospital after delivering her child, "You can't give that baby away. That's my grandchild!" But there was no offer of a house, of money to help raise that child. The birthfather was there and was being very supportive. He commented, "The people who are trying to tell her what to do never offer any help at all. They don't come in and talk with a counselor; they just expect Jane to bend their way."

"You see it over and over. 'Adoption is not an option, but we're not going to help you solve the problems,'" Kennedy said.

Birthmother Is Adopted

Alice and Tom adopted Roseanne 16 years ago when she was an infant. They knew adoption from the other side. They knew indeed that adoption is an option, but agreed to support Roseanne, whatever her decision:

Tom: I certainly did give adoption a lot of thought, but I knew from the beginning that Roseanne would have to make the final decision. I decided if she kept the baby or if she released, I would support her decision. I wanted the baby, but I didn't want another family. I was there to be her support in whatever she decided. I was leaning more toward the adoption for her sake and the baby's sake, probably because we had adopted Roseanne. We were thrilled to get her, of course, but I also felt her birthmother had a better chance because she made this decision.

Adoption is not second class.

Alice: I think we had a different perspective because we had been on the other end of adoption. We knew the joy, we knew the excitement, all those wonderful positive things that adoption can bring. Adoption isn't second class.

Tom: It's not that you don't love the child, it's because you love the child so much, you want the best for that child. There are going to be a lot of tears down the road, a lot of hurt inside. We have to separate the needs of the child from our emotions. That's how I tried to encourage Roseanne the entire time. The child has a whole life ahead.

Alice: Roseanne had already worked all of this through in her own mind.

Tom: This is the most I've thought about it since the baby left. This is terribly emotional, and I wasn't expecting the emotions to come back so strong *(his voice is breaking)*. I look back on it as making the best of a tough time.

Father's Parents Are Supportive

*If the birthmother and her parents are making an adoption plan but the birthfather's parents are adamantly opposed to adoption, working out the differences between the two families may be very difficult. This was **not** a problem for Roseanne and her family. Doug's parents were also supportive of adoption. Beth, Doug's mother, explained:*

We agreed with Roseanne's parents that adoption was an option as long as the baby was placed with a family of born-again Christians. Having that much control seemed to help us, knowing that this child would be placed in an environment close to ours.

As far as taking the baby ourselves, that didn't seem a good idea. Neither was it a good option for Roseanne's parents. I have never felt it was a healthy atmosphere for a child to be reared with an unwed mother and her parents. How can that child get a clear picture of what family is all about?

So many things come down to what each of us can live with. I really feel adoption is an option not considered adequately.

Moving from Fantasy to Reality

The need for counseling is mentioned over and over by the birthfamilies who share their experiences here. Pregnancy counselors, of course, also feel strongly that counseling is helpful in almost any case of too-early pregnancy.

About two weeks after Chris was born, 16-year-old Stacy listened as her father talked about the months before she delivered. Then Ted asked his daughter, "What do you think you would have done if you hadn't gone to the agency and made all those decisions?" Stacy replied:

I probably would have kept her. The thought never crossed my mind except that Ed was adopted. He didn't want to give up his baby and I didn't, so we were thinking,

"Oh, we'll keep the baby." His mom doesn't work, so we thought she could take care of the baby while I'd go to school. Some day, after I'm out of school, we'd get married and live happily ever after.

If I hadn't gone to the agency I might have said, "We're keeping the baby, and when Ed graduates, we'll get married." I probably would have kept the baby, and I don't know what would have happened. I don't think I would ever have asked for counseling. It's easy to look to the first year. That's the easy one.

With Angela, my counselor, we started looking further ahead into the future. "What are you going to do?" she asked. I didn't want to live at home with my parents forever.

I thought, "Well, I could get welfare," but that didn't appeal to me. For awhile that was the only option. So if Ed gets a job at 18, what kind of a job can he get? It wasn't realistic.

---

*I got very serious about adoption
and set my mind to it.*

I thought, "Guy, this poor kid is going to grow up struggling." She wouldn't see me because I knew I'd have to go to work, get some kind of job, a career, to support her. She'd have to be with a babysitter, and I didn't want that. I grew up with my mom here, and I knew I couldn't provide that kind of closeness for my child. Of course I changed my mind a million times.

I went back and forth a lot, and I finally said, "This is what I want to do." I got very serious about adoption and set my mind to it. We sat down and looked at families. I had been envisioning this perfect family that would jump right out and say, "Take me, I'm yours." But I didn't see that.

Then Angela showed me Ric and Peggy's resume, and I fell hopelessly in love with them. Ric was dark haired, they were tall, her hair was dark like mine, they fit. Their house was incredible, they had horses, and I always wanted horses. Angela read me their autobiography, and I was hooked. She gave me a picture to bring home, and I told my best friend, "I found them, I found them."

Angela called that night and said, "Ric and Peggy are ready to adopt, they have a picture of you, and they are totally excited." I cried, I was so happy. I called my mom at work, and I tried to call Ed, but he wasn't home.

So we met Ric and Peggy, and of course I was nervous. I said, "Mom, I have to drive, I have to have something to do." I came in, and I heard them talking. Angela said, "They're here. I'll go get them."

I thought, "They won't look like their pictures," but they looked exactly like their pictures. Peggy was bubbly and Ric was quiet much the way it is with Ed and me. We had a great time.

I met again with Peggy the following week and we talked. We found we had a lot in common, personality-wise. For example, I told Peggy that when I get mad, I get loud. And she said, "I do too, and Ric hates it."

Becky – Cooperative Adoption

Lucia, mother of 16-year-old Becky, is a strong advocate of counseling. Because of the counseling she received at Parenting Resources, Tustin, California, Lucia is developing a support group for birthgrandparents. She shared the pain she experienced because of her daughter's pregnancy:

The morning after Becky told us she was pregnant I called an adoption agency. I told them I was afraid Becky was going to have an abortion. A counselor came out that morning and Becky agreed to talk with her.

At this agency, we learned, Becky could look through adoptive couple resumes and give her opinion, but she couldn't have the final say in choosing a family for her child. The agency would do that. *(Many agencies now encourage the birthparents to make the final selection of adoptive parents for their baby.)*

Apparently with this agency, the baby wouldn't go
directly to the adoptive couple, but would spend a few days
with a foster family. Becky didn't want that, so independent adoption seemed preferable to us. *(Many adoption
agencies do place babies with their adoptive parents
directly from the hospital.)*

Becky grew up fast. She took control of the situation
and made plans for her baby. I think she did very well. She
sought out the counseling. She decided she wanted open
cooperative adoption because she wanted continuing
contact with her child, so she called Parenting Resources in
Tuestin.

Becky called the first two adoptive couples and interviewed them herself. Neither couple clicked with her. For
the third couple, she asked me to call first to ask about a
couple of things not on their resume. I did, and suddenly I
was involved.

The day I called Linda, she was baking Christmas
cookies. I said, "I know this may sound very rigid, but we
need some more information." I asked about their religion,
and if she was willing to stay home with this child for a
year or so. Then I said, "Please don't get too excited. I
have to get back to my daughter and see if she wants to
meet you."

I liked what Linda said, and found myself hoping Becky
would choose them. I've been told by counselors that I
need to take myself out of the middle and just be there. It's
a difficult position to be in for a birthgrandmother. You
want this grandchild to have the best life possible, and at
the same time you want to be supportive of your daughter.

Becky asked me to call Linda back and tell her she
wanted to meet them. Two days later Linda and Bill came
to our home and visited with Becky. I stayed upstairs for a
couple of hours, and then Becky called me down to
meet them.

A few days later Becky called Linda and said, "I've
decided I'd like you to be my child's adoptive parents."
The next day she received a huge bouquet of long-
stemmed red roses with a Christmas card. After that we

were together a few times as families, mostly in each others' homes. They also started going to the support group for adoptive parents at Parenting Resources.

The first two couples Becky interviewed were obviously quite well-to-do. She was thinking, "I want the best for my child. These two couples sound rich." But then she started realizing that money really wasn't the main issue. The people she chose live in a rather modest home, but Becky felt this home would be filled with love. Something clicked, and it wasn't the fact that they had money.

> *Every avenue needs to be explored,*
> *every option discussed*
> *before that final decision is made.*

Counseling is the key. If you're in this situation, get as much counseling as you can, read everything you can find to educate you about your options. You also need to talk as a family, with your daughter, between husband and wife – always keeping in mind that your daughter will make the decision. Let her know that you'll support her, really and truly support her in whatever she decides.

I keep slipping and saying the decision was ours, and it almost was a family decision. I know Becky was greatly influenced by our feelings. She felt all along that adoption was her choice, but I know we could have influenced her so her decision would have been to keep the baby.

You need to explore all options, and you get so sick of discussing it. You get to the point where you're almost counseled out. But it's so important. Every avenue needs to be explored, every option discussed before that final decision is made.

We tried hard not to let other people influence our decision. In fact, we didn't let a lot of relatives know about Becky's pregnancy because we didn't want anyone else in the family influencing her.

Adoption for somebody in our situation is not an attractive option for most people. We are middle class,

possibly upper middle class. Money is not a problem. We
could have raised this child very nicely. Actually I think
this made our decision harder because we had to stick with
what would be best for the baby, not what we could afford.

A lot of our friends and family would look at us and say,
"Why is she doing this? It doesn't make any sense. You
can raise this baby." But ultimately it had to be Becky's
decision. She had to decide her baby's future.

"She's Not a Tramp"

When Anne learned about her 13-year-old daughter Joan's
pregnancy only five weeks before the baby was born, she
panicked briefly. Then Anne began helping Joan face the
realities ahead. They agreed to make an adoption plan, but Anne
was determined that the baby's adoptive parents think highly of
their child's birthmother:

There was never a question of abortion. I feel every
woman has a right to do as she thinks best, but I'm not big
on abortion. There are too many people out there who want
and need babies. My niece and nephew are both adopted,
and the man I worked for has two adopted children.
Several other friends have adopted children so I know the
joy adopted children bring to a family.

There was never a question in our minds of keeping the
baby. I had discussed it with Joan before we went in to see
the doctor. At 13 she was very mature, and I explained to
her the pros and the cons.

Joan agreed immediately, and said that she felt the baby
would be much better off in a home where there were two
parents who were married and really wanted to raise
a child.

We discussed this with the doctor, and learned he was
an Ob-Gyn who also specialized in infertility. He had five
couples at that time who desperately wanted babies. He
had one couple especially in mind, and we agreed they
would be given a chance to accept this baby.

I told the doctor we wanted an open adoption, that we didn't want this to be a closed issue. I want the adoptive family to know who the mother was, that she was a young girl who made a mistake. She is extremely intelligent, and I want the parents to know she is not a tramp, that she comes from a good family.

If they can't agree to that, I told him, I want another family who will accept us. I want this to be an open adoption. The doctor called them, and they called us. They live in this area. We had several discussions and the husband said, "We already love you so much for what you're doing for us. We know how hard it is for you to do this, and we want you to know how much it means to us to have this opportunity to have a child and to raise it."

It was a difficult time in all of our lives. I guess the thing that hurt me the most was the way Joan's friends reacted. Not her good friends – they stood by her, and they never judged her. I finally took her out of school, and she had a home teacher.

I kept her with me, and thank God I was home to be with her. I took her everywhere I went, and I'm still proud of her. It was a hard time for both of us, but I felt the worst about what Joan had to go through.

Moving a baby from one family to another is a crisis situation for both families.

Simply choosing an adoptive family through a doctor or a lawyer is risky primarily because of the probable lack of counseling for either the birthfamily or the adoptive family. Moving a baby from one family to another is a crisis situation for both families, and a caring, sensitive professional counselor can help both families deal with the adoption crisis and its aftermath.

Follow-up services are extremely important. Anne's request for an open adoption was reasonable, but she needs to understand that contact with the adoptive couple after the adoption is

*finalized has no legal support. If the birthfamily is working with
an adoption agency with good follow-up services, however, the
agency can intercede if the adoptive family appears not to be
going along with the agreement for contact with the birthfamily.
While the agency counselor can't force the contact, she can
certainly encourage it.*

*Sharon Kaplan, Parenting Resources, compares birthgrand-
parents' need for counseling services with birthfathers' needs.
"If we didn't ask to see birthfathers, we didn't see them," she
recalls. "Now I'm saying counseling services are available for
grandmothers, and they're coming in.*

*"Of all the pregnant women we're seeing this month aged 13-
22, about three-fourths of the birthgrandmas are either seeing
me or another staff member for counseling. We're also seeing a
lot of grandmothers at our monthly adoption support group
meetings.*

*"In fact," Kaplan continues, "we see the birthgrandparents
long after the birthmother has gone on to college and is getting
on with her life. I'm wondering if the grandmother tends to have
a delayed grief response because she feels she has to support
her daughter through the pregnancy and afterward. Then when
the daughter moves on, the grandmother's grief is finally able to
surface. Agency resources are slim, and they have more work
than they can handle. Outreach to grandmothers isn't talked
about a great deal.*

*"The amount of counseling offered to birthgrandparents
varies a great deal from agency to agency. Many say, 'If a
birthgrandparent asks for counseling, we won't turn her away.'
But there is very little seeking them out. There's a lot of lip
service to their need for help, but not much push," Kaplan
concludes.*

5

MAKING
THE DECISION

Ideally, parents of a pregnant teenager will support her
during her pregnancy and afterward in whatever decision she
makes. It is their daughter who will experience the intense
feelings of approaching motherhood. It is she who will suffer the
pain of losing her baby if she makes an adoption plan and
releases her child.

If she keeps her baby, it is she who will (should) take the
responsibility of parenting – first a tiny infant, then a toddler,
preschooler, and on until her child reaches adulthood some
eighteen years later. The baby won't be her parents' responsibility (although some grandparents do assume the role of
parenting the baby).

Accepting Her Decision

Often, when I talk with a pregnant teenager and her mother, I
explain that most of the girls in our Teen Mother Program keep
their babies to rear themselves. However, each year several

*girls make and carry out an adoption plan for their babies. It's
extremely important, I point out, that we accept totally each
other's decisions. No one is ever to say to a birthmother, "How
could you possibly give your baby away?" Neither is anyone to
give a student a hard time for choosing to rear her child herself.*

*Once, as I was explaining this to Alexis, a new student, her
mother interrupted me. Pointing at her daughter, she said
indignantly, "Well, if she ever even thought about giving that
baby away, I'd kill her!"*

Alexis obviously had no choice. She could not **choose** *to be a
parent. It was a role she must assume. "Parental pressure to
keep is overwhelming," commented Charlotte De Armond,
former Public Affairs Director of Children's Home Society of
California.*

*"So often it's 'my grandchild' we're talking about, without
much thought as to whether or not a 15-year-old mother is best
for that grandchild," she continued. "Sometimes, too, the
teenager's mother is getting to the age when she can't have her
own baby, so she wants to have this one."*

*"I have never known a girl who relinquished her infant at
birth if her parents wanted her to keep it," a CHS social worker
reported, "but it does go the other way – I've known several
girls whose parents wanted them to release the baby for
adoption, but they didn't."*

Birthparent Must Decide

*Neither Georgia nor Eric could imagine their 16-year-old
daughter, Lilia, parenting her child. Georgia would have liked
to keep the baby, but Eric was adamantly opposed. Together
they struggled with their own decision – to allow Lilia to decide
for herself:*

Eric's first thought was adoption. He said to Lilia,
"Well, what are you going to do?"

"What do you mean?" She assumed she'd keep the
baby, and he was upset.

"You're a child, you can't raise a baby," he told her.

At first I thought, "We just can't do that. We can't give

up my daughter's child for adoption." I don't know why I
felt that way, but I guess because it was a part of her. I
went through a period of thinking, "How can it be possible
that this child is going to have a baby?" It blew my mind.

---

*Finally I realized
that though Lilia is only 16,
she is going to be a mother.*

There were times when I put her down for it. She'd do a
household task and not do it right. Once she cooked some
pork chops and they were half raw, and I said, "You have
so much to learn. You're not ready to be a mother." I'd say
hurtful things, and then I'd go back and apologize.

Finally I realized that though Lilia is only 16, she *is*
going to be a mother. She can be a mother, and if she
decides to keep the baby, she can do it and make mistakes
as I have.

Once when we were riding in the car, I said, "What do
you think about adoption?"

"I couldn't do that," she said.

"Why not?"

"I couldn't adopt my baby out."

"Why not?"

"I couldn't. That's an unloving thing."

I was shocked. I said, "How could you possibly say
that? Your birthmother loved you so much, and she knew
she couldn't afford another child. She couldn't give you
what you needed so she decided to give you up for adoption. Can you imagine how much strength that took, how
much love?" And I think it really sunk in.

Because I've worked on an abortion hot line, I have
some information on counseling girls thinking about
adoption. I had a three- or four-page questionnaire, so as a
start, I gave this to Lilia. She didn't want to think about
adoption at all. The questionnaire has both sides – Should I
keep my baby? Should I place for adoption? How about
getting up in the morning, getting ready for school, with

a baby? How about dates? And the other side, how would I
feel if I made an adoption plan?

I think talking with other people who have been through
the same thing also helped. Amy (adoption counselor)
suggested Lilia go out with Erin, a birthmother who had
recently joined our church. Erin was 23, an adult, but still
young enough to relate to my daughter. They went out to
dinner together and talked for several hours. Lilia was
surprised that Erin could still smile and be happy after
placing her baby four months earlier.

As you know, you can't tell your children what you
think is best for them. . .well, you can, but they won't
listen to you. But sometimes they'll listen to someone else.
I offered Lilia a couple of books written for birthparents –
Dear Birthmother (Corona Publishing, 1981) and *Pregnant
Too Soon* (Morning Glory Press, 1988). I think she
read them.

I finally came to grips with the fact that I couldn't tell
her what to do. I told my husband I couldn't make Lilia
give this baby up because if we do, she may get pregnant
again.

I've found this happens with girls who abort. Sometimes
they replace that baby. So I thought it would be worse if
she released, then put us through this again. Far worse, she
might end up hating us for the rest of our lives, and we
certainly didn't want that.

Lilia is finding lots of opposition to adoption.

It took a long time. My husband was resistant, and I had
to be the counselor to him and to my daughter. (We've
been married eight years.)

He kept saying, "She can't be a mother." But he finally
agreed she should be the one to make up her mind.

That's one thing parents of pregnant teens need to
understand. It's hard – you have a child and these are the
rules of the house – homework, phone privileges taken

away, etc., yet here is this child having a baby, and you
have no control over it. You can't say, "You're pregnant,
we'll take your phone away."

Lilia is finding lots of opposition to adoption. Two
weeks ago she went out with my first husband, her father.
They visited an aunt and this aunt said, "I'll take care of
your baby. When you're ready, you can come back and get
him." It's very hard for me not to call back and say, "Don't
you know what you're doing to Lilia and to her baby?"
That's so thoughtless.

About half-way through her pregnancy, Lilia decided to
enroll in our district's special school for pregnant girls.
Even there she found no support for adoption. No one
talked about it.

I can't believe how ignorant the world is about adoption.

They had speakers on all sorts of other issues – but
nothing on adoption. Lilia said she mentioned once that she
might consider adoption. Because of the other girls'
reactions, she vowed never to do that again.

"How can you do such a cruel thing?" one asked.

Another said, "Adoption is worse than abortion."

Lilia just looked at her and said, "How can you say
that?" Lilia's smart enough to know that's not true.

I can't believe how ignorant the world is about adoption.
Even my mother, brother, close friends can't seem to
understand that adoption is an option. Even when I remind
them that Lilia is adopted, they gloss it over. I think they
pretend that she was born to us.

This has taught me – I have almost never thought about
Lilia's birthmother, but now I think about her a lot. I think
of all the pain she must have gone through and all the tears
she must have shed. I have a real guilt complex for not
thinking of her feelings long ago.

When Lilia was two, her birthmother's older sister came
into town. She called me and wanted to see Lilia. I said,

"No, not after all this time. Don't even go past my house."
I was outraged. I didn't stop to think that Lilia's
birthmother has feelings, too, very strong feelings.

As soon as I can, I'm going to try to contact Lilia's
birthmother, send pictures, and say, "Thank you." How
courageous she must have been and how much love she
had to let us have Lilia.

Lilia Shares Her Experience

Lilia: When I first found out I was pregnant, I assumed
I was going to keep the baby. I told my mother I was
pregnant a week after I found out, but only because we
were going skiing, and I didn't want to go.

She asked me what I was going to do, and I said, "This
is mine and no one is going to take it away from me."

Then my mom said, "Well, you have an option to put it
up for adoption."

"Oh?" I said. I never really thought about it. It was like
someone had to tell me that for me to think about it.

Then I said, "No, I don't want to do that." But I just kept
thinking and thinking about it. Then I talked to a friend at
church, and she said, "Would you like to talk to someone
who has given her baby up for adoption?"

I really didn't want to, but my mom said, "Why don't
you talk to her?" And that right there changed my mind
completely.

Erin (birthmother) was happy, and I said, "How can you
be happy?" We met for dinner, and we stayed there for
about five hours talking and talking.

She told me about her whole experience, and that really
shocked me. That changed my mind, talking to someone
who had been through it and was OK. That's how I chose
adoption.

When I went home I already knew, but I didn't tell my
mom right away. Just talking with someone else made a
big difference. Mom and Dad suggested they'd like me to
give the baby up for adoption, but they said they would

support me either way. I think that helped. I needed
someone who could advise me, who could suggest which
would be best.

The questionnaire my mom gave me was good, too, and
so was the one Amy gave me. Now when I get real
depressed, I look at them and that helps me.

Erin went through Calvary Chapel, so I said, "OK, I
want to do that." I prayed about it a lot. Then I went down
there just to look and to talk to Amy, the counselor. I went
through perhaps 30 files, but I couldn't find what I wanted.
I wanted a Mexican family, and there were none. Amy said
they were going to have a seminar soon with a bunch of
new parents, so I said, "OK, I'll wait."

Two weeks later my mom called Amy back and made
an appointment for me to see her again. Mom picked me
up from school and said, "You have this appointment." I
should have gotten mad because she didn't ask me, but
when she said, "You don't have to go," I said, "OK,
whatever."

I needed to meet them to make sure
they'd be OK for my baby.

Amy had some new files, and we looked at about ten. I
found one that looked nice and put it aside. Then I found
another one I liked. So I picked from these two. I took the
information home to show my dad, and it sat in our front
room for nearly a month. So what do we do next?

Amy called me, and I said, "I've picked Maggie and Al
and I really like them."

"Next, you meet them," she said.

"I don't want to."

"Then what do you want to do?" And I realized I needed
to meet them to make sure they'd be OK for my baby. So
Amy set up an appointment with Maggie and Al. She and
my mom went with me, but my dad didn't go. He's concerned and wants to be supportive, but he's kind of staying
out of it.

We met for dinner, but no one wanted to eat because we were all so nervous.

I really liked Maggie and Al. My mom said to them, "We'll call you if Lilia wants you to be the parents."

"Mom, yes, I want them," I whispered to her. I wanted to tell them, but they had already walked out. So I told Amy, "These are the parents."

"Are you sure?"

"Yes, yes, I'm sure."

And my mom said, "Are you sure?"

I said, "Yes," and Amy said I should tell them, but I didn't know how.

Maggie and Al were already almost to their car by now, and we went running after them. Amy yelled real loud, "Wait!"

My mom was crying, and I was saying, "What do I say? What do I do?"

Al and Maggie stopped, and as we went up to them, I said, "Amy, what do I say? What do I say?"

"Just tell them."

Finally I said, "I want you to be the parents of my baby," and they cried and they cried.

We're planning to keep in touch.
They'll send me pictures.

Since then we've gone out to dinner several times, and they've met my dad. Maggie will be in the delivery room with me. Maggie's church is having a baby shower for her next week, and it makes me all excited to see them.

I'm kind of thinking I'm really just babysitting. That makes it easier.

We're planning to keep in touch. They'll send me pictures, and Al said last week, when we went out to dinner, that when the baby is 18, we could have a little reunion.

I said, "That would be neat." I want always to keep in contact so they'll know where I am.

Pregnant Too Soon: Adoption Is an Option includes a four-page questionnaire (pages 196-199) designed to help a pregnant teenager decide whether she (or he) is ready to parent at this time. You may want to suggest that your daughter consider these questions, perhaps answer them in writing, as a guide to organizing her thoughts. If the baby's father is involved in the decision-making, they may prefer to go over the questions together.

Parenting is great – if it's the right time. Do they feel this is the right time for them?

Complete Honesty Is Important

Claire Priester, House of Ruth Ministries, Downey, California, stresses that parents need to decide what kind of support they can give. Even if they've decided adoption is best, they need to allow their daughter to make that decision.

"Most girls, given the options, will make a good decision if they know what their resources are," Priester insists. "Parents need to let her know where they'll fit in. Either they will let her live at home with the baby or they won't. If they'll help financially, how much, and how long will the support last?"

Knowing the specifics will help the young mother-to-be make a good plan. It's the girl who doesn't know what her parents will do who doesn't make a good decision, according to Priester. Priester has known families who say they'll help, but after the baby is born they say, "You have to get a job." The young mother thought she'd be going to school.

"Too many people don't consider their options. For many, babies stay in families. In effect, they're saying to their daughter, "You made your bed, now lie in it," says Priester. "I think some children are damaged because they really should not have been kept by their birthfamilies.

"On the other hand," Priester continues, "other parents think adoption is the only option for a young teenager and that may not be best for their daughter.

"I think either extreme is wrong. It's wrong to assume that either one is the only possibility. You need to walk through the decision-making process. I don't buy it when somebody walks in here and says, 'I want to give up my baby.' I say, 'Have you looked at your situation?'"

She made her decision based on inaccurate information.

Catherine Monserrat, Family Therapist, Seattle, Washington, also highly recommends that families be clear with their daughter about what they are willing to do. Two of Monserrat's clients felt they couldn't go home with their babies. Yet one learned later that she could have come home. Twila, the other client, was told by her parents that she could have visited them with her baby. Twila had thought they meant she could never go back if she kept her baby.

"Twila feels she made her decision based on inaccurate information," Monserrat explained. "I don't think she really regrets the adoption now because she has seen her baby with his parents, and she feels good about that meeting. Her rage was about having been lied to and manipulated.

"I don't care what the justification is, I don't think it's fair to lie to somebody," Monserrat concludes.

Discussing these things thoroughly, then making a contract together before the baby is born can be helpful. How much will the parents babysit? Who will really be in charge of this child, the young mother or father? Her parents? His parents?

Taking the young parent(s)-to-be shopping will help her/them see how expensive baby things are. Go beyond babyhood. What will it cost three to five years from now? Young people who really know what they have to work with can make a better decision.

Some Parents Push Adoption

Mary Struck, Hope Services, Seattle, Washington, often works with birthgrandparents along with their daughters. She feels strongly that grandparents need permission to recognize their own rights.

"We've had more than one birthgrandmother tell her 15-year-old daughter that she couldn't come home with the baby. 'If you bring this baby home, you must move out and start your own life,'" Struck recalls. "We support them because the grandparents have rights too, and one of those rights is they don't have to raise their daughter's child.

"The adoption is not likely to go through if the grandmother sends mixed messages," Struck continues. "It's hard for a young girl to buck her mother. She still needs her mom a lot, needs her approval, needs attention from her. If her mom says, "This is our child, a member of our family," the birthmother won't go through with the adoption."

Birthgrandmothers sometimes have a harder time with relinquishment than the birthmoms do, especially if the teenager is very young, according to Struck. "I've wondered about that. I wonder if perhaps the birthmom at 15 has nothing to relate relinquishment to. She has never been a mother, but her mother knows what she's giving up," Struck says.

"Often it's the first grandchild, and it's supposed to be a very special event for those parents. Of course birthparents hurt when the baby goes, but so do the grandparents. In these cases, it's difficult to be supportive of their daughter's decision to relinquish," she concludes.

With teen parents, rejection is a very common thing.

Janet Cravins, Lutheran Social Service of Texas, agrees with Struck that teenagers who place are those whose parents are supportive of adoption. Carried to the extreme, however, she feels this can be very hurtful.

"Having her family say, 'You can't bring your baby home' is very rejecting to a teenager," Cravens points out. "With teen parents, rejection is a very common thing. In a counseling relationship, that often comes up as a big issue – how rejected

by their parents they feel. I don't find that's at all helpful to that young birthmother – to tell her she can't come home with her baby. Instead, families need to get some help in working out their differences."

Susan, barely 16, desperately wanted a child. Her parents, however, were determined that she not become a mother yet. This is her story:

"We have a student who wants to talk to you. Can you come over this morning?" The caller was a counselor from a neighboring high school.

Thirty minutes later I met Susan. I soon learned she was the girl I had heard about the previous week. She was pregnant and her folks were insisting she get an abortion.

Susan, close to tears, started talking.

"My parents can't stand Carlos — they think that because his parents don't speak English and aren't rich, they don't amount to anything. But I love him!" she wailed. We talked for an hour. Susan told me about her family, her relationship with Carlos, and how she didn't want an abortion.

I heard a few days later that Susan had run away from home and was living with Carlos and his parents. Four days later she was home, and the next day her parents took her to the hospital for an abortion. (Illegal? Only if Susan didn't sign the release form. Parents have no legal right to insist their daughter get an abortion, but from a realistic standpoint, it can – and does – sometimes happen.)

> *We've done everything for Susan,
> and look what's happened.*

Less than a year later Susan was in my class. She was pregnant again, but she was no longer with Carlos. Because of her parents, Susan and Carlos had split up after she had the abortion. Now Susan was pregnant by someone else, a boy she scarcely knew and insisted she didn't care about. By the time she told her parents, it was too late for another abortion.

When I visited her home after she had enrolled in the class, Susan excused herself. Her mother and I talked. Mrs. Lacey was a lovely, well-groomed woman in her late forties, perhaps fifties. She had three married children who lived nearby. She worked for an insurance agency.

"We just don't understand," she said tearfully. "We've done everything for Susan, and look what's happened. We were terribly hurt last year when she was involved with that worthless boy – and his family made no attempt to stop them. We were relieved when that was over – we could start again. We told Susan we wouldn't hold that against her. If she would work hard in school and do her best to get along at home, we'd never mention that mess.

"And we thought things were going pretty well. Then three weeks ago she sprang this on us. And this time she doesn't even care about the boy! We can't believe it. And she wants to keep the baby. . .

She was still hoping she could live at home after her baby's birth.

"We've told her she can't bring a baby back here. If she keeps that baby, she'll have to live someplace else. She says she would take care of it, but I know better.

"I know how she doesn't take responsibility. I know I'd end up having that baby, and I've already had my family. That part of my life is gone, and I certainly don't want to start over."

Susan continued coming to school, but she seemed more and more depressed as the weeks went by. At first she had told me how much she wanted this baby, that no one could talk her out of keeping it. She was still hoping she could live at home after her baby's birth.

About a month before delivery, she admitted to herself that her parents meant it. She really couldn't go home with her baby.

She decided she wasn't ready to survive by herself. Her parents talked to their lawyer, and an independent adoption was arranged.

Susan delivered a little boy one cold February night. She said she didn't want to see her son. She signed the consent for release from the hospital, and the baby was placed immediately with his new family.

Susan returned to her other school. She graduated from high school in June. A few months later she called to tell me she was pregnant again. "And this time I'm finally going to have a baby of my own," she told me.

Those two years were difficult times for Susan. She will always remember the two children she doesn't have – the one she lost unwillingly through abortion, and the other through adoption. Apparently there was no "good" solution to the conflict between her desire to have a child and her parents' determination that she not become a mother at 16.

Susan's case is not unusual. Statistics show a high pregnancy repeat rate among girls who feel they are pushed into either abortion or adoption against their wishes.

Telling her she can keep the baby
but she can't take it home
isn't giving her a choice if she's 15.

Jennifer Stebbins, Christian Adoption and Family Services, Anaheim, California, wants parents to offer realistic choices to their daughters.

"Telling her she can keep the baby, but she can't take it home isn't giving her a choice if she's 15," Stebbins points out. "I think they have to get behind her and support her, let her know she has the freedom to choose. With that freedom, she can make a more rational decision.

"I like the family to spell it out to her. If she absolutely can't bring the baby home, they should make that clear to her even though she really won't have much choice. They should be as

specific as they can – 'I'll babysit one day each week. You'll be responsible for your baby the rest of the time.' That's much better than either 'We aren't babysitting' or 'we'll help you, dear. Of course we'll babysit.' Tell her what the limits will be," advises Stebbins.

Stacy Makes Her Decision

Stacy felt at first that her parents were pushing adoption. Then she found her friends pushing keeping. Stacy was determined not to make a decision based on how other people felt. She knew this had to be her decision, and she finally decided to place Chris for adoption.

After Chris was born, Stacy's parents discussed the adoption decision-making:

Ted: Right in the beginning I told Stacy I thought she should consider adoption for her sake and for her baby's sake. And, although I didn't say it, for my sake and her mother's sake. She didn't like the idea at all, and I wondered afterward if I had come on too strong. Later she said, "I may not do this simply because you're insisting." Then she talked to kids at school, and everyone there told her she should keep. She said then she might adopt because they told her not to.

I was convinced that having a baby here in the house wasn't the thing to do, but if that was what Stacy wanted, we'd deal with it.

Stacy agreed to go to the agency, and Angela did a terrific job of counseling.

Mary Lou: At the agency they don't pressure one way or another. They give you both sides. They gave Stacy homework to do. If you're planning to keep the baby, how do you intend to provide for it? We had to go shopping and price out a layette. Stacy had other questions to think about: Are you getting support from the birthfather? From your parents? How do you think you're going to feel when your mother steps in and tells you what to do with your baby? Angela presented all these problems.

One thing I was adamant about – I wasn't going to make a decision for my daughter other than being sure she got to the doctor and that she got counseling. But I told Ted we couldn't make the adoption/keeping decision for her. She had to decide what was going to happen in her life.

What kind of job could she get to support a baby?

If Stacy was willing to make the sacrifice involved in raising a child, fine. But we would let her know what our limitations were, how far we could go in supporting another child.

Sometimes a girl will say, "Well, Mom will help," but she may not think about how much it costs for food, clothes, health care.

Little ones are easy, but within two years your precious little baby is a child who needs a great deal of time and resources.

I told Stacy we were limited, but she would have a roof over her head. I said she could have one year. If she decided to keep the baby, I would take one year off from work and take care of the baby while she finished high school.

We aren't poor, but we need my income. I said I could give her a year, but what would she do after that year was up? A baby is sweet and loveable, but there are medical expenses, clothes. What kind of job could she get to support a baby?

Ted: Once Stacy decided, she picked a family, and everything went so smoothly from then on it was almost the classic adoption. When we met the parents, there was almost instant rapport.

They liked us and we liked them. When the baby was born we were all at the hospital. They took pictures of us, and we took pictures of them. Stacy put together a photo album of the whole event.

Mary Lou: It all came together. We feel perhaps it's because we're a Christian family, and this was meant to be. Adoption probably doesn't always work this smoothly. The birthmother might go through more trauma. Stacy went back and forth with her decision. But one thing she did was make a commitment in her heart that she would not get a family involved until she had decided to go ahead with the adoption decision.

Once the family was there, that sealed her decision. She didn't want to be responsible for crushing their hopes. So she committed herself to the adoption before the baby was born.

That's a very mature attitude for a 17-year-old, and we're very proud of her. I know it was hard for her to let another family rear her baby.

Ted: Some people aren't able to do this, to give the baby up. But then they have to decide how far they'll go to raise this baby. If you have a teenage daughter, there are going to be some conflicts. With a baby involved, there has to be more communication between the daughter and her parents. Will the young mother rear her child, or will her parents do it? As a family, you have to decide how these issues will be handled.

The young mother has to know what she'll be expected to do. Will Mom and Dad be responsible for her child? We didn't want to do that. I know Stacy is a strong individual, and she wouldn't want Mom to tell her what to do. There would be clashes, and we talked about that. We also had to think about making space for the baby, and we had to consider Stacy's little brother's feelings.

What Is Rational?

It's a fine line between "supporting" someone in her decision versus applying pressure for her to follow your wishes. Attempts at being "rational" can be difficult. After all, what is "rational" about a mother giving up her baby? On the other hand, what is "rational" about a tenth grader assuming the role of mother?

*In our society, there are risks either way. There is the risk of
real emotional trauma for the young birthmother if she releases
her baby for adoption. There are risks of no job skills, not
enough education, no time to have fun for the teenager who
chooses too-early parenthood.*

So what's a parent to do?

*No one can tell you what is best in your situation. Was
Susan's mother wrong absolutely to forbid her daughter to bring
the baby home? Would Mrs. Lacey have been "right" if she had
decided to help Susan cope with motherhood by taking over the
responsibility for her grandchild?*

There is no easy answer.

*Susan might have fared better if she had had a chance to look
at her options, to make a choice based on what was possible in
her family.*

*She had no one except herself to care for a baby. Could she
have coped? Possibly. Possibly not. Discussing her situation
with a trained adoption counselor might have helped Susan look
at her various alternatives. Instead, her family simply called
their lawyer to set up the adoption.*

She might have decided
a father was also needed
in her parenting picture.

---

*Accepting Susan's blithe "I can take care of it – I love
babies" might not be practical. Encouraging her to "try" could
be very hard on her baby. If she found she couldn't cope, the
trauma of releasing her baby later would have been even
greater than it was at birth.*

*Jim Mead, founder of For Kids Sake, Inc., Brea, California,
an organization devoted to the prevention of child abuse, has a
unique suggestion for parents trying to toilet-train their toddler.
He recommends they "rent a kid" for a weekend. The require-
ment is that the "rented kid" will take that toddler with him/her
every time s/he goes to the bathroom. By Sunday night, Mead
insists, that toddler will be potty trained!*

*Renting a baby is **not** advisable.*

However, Susan might have spent two or three weeks with a family with a new baby. (She had no younger brothers and sisters. Her babysitting experience consisted mainly of evening assignments with sleeping babies.) Most young mothers would welcome help.

Perhaps Susan could have spent a weekend taking full responsibility for a toddler. Then she might have had a clearer idea of what it takes to parent a child in the throes of saying "No" to everything, a child who runs constantly, and requires total supervision.

Susan's reaction to her "fostering" experiences might have been positive. Perhaps it would have reinforced her desire to be a mother herself.

At the same time, it might have helped her mother realize Susan was, indeed, capable of being a mother in spite of her youth and singleness.

Or Susan might have found the constant care of either the infant or toddler exhausting. She might have decided that, much as she wanted a child, perhaps that was not the time. She might have decided a father was also needed in her parenting picture.

That fact of constant care-giving is an interesting aspect of parenting. Young mothers mention often that everyone – parents and friends – promise to help take care of the baby. Before it's born, they can hardly wait to babysit for her. During the first few months the babysitting offers are still frequent.

When her baby becomes a crawling, into-everything youngster some eight months later, the offers to care for her child often dwindle to almost nothing.

As Sarah put it in speaking of eight-month-old Joanna and the friends who no longer wanted to babysit, "I guess she's just too old."

Reality Therapy May Help

Bonnie Adkins-DeJong, Bethany Christian Services, Bellflower, California, advocates reality therapy. "When someone tells me she plans to be a doctor, and that having a child won't interfere, I say, 'That's great, you're going to be a doctor. Let's *see how you're going to get there. Let's not have surprises along the way. You're a sophomore in high school and you're looking at medical school. That's 14 years, and with a child, it may take 17.'*

"'Well, that's no problem,' she says.

"'How old will you be then?'

"'That's okay.'

"My goal is that if she parents, she be the best parent possible. How will she do this and reach her goals?

"Most of the girls say, 'It's not important. I'm going to keep my baby.'

"'Well, what are you going to do? What is important for your baby to have? This is what welfare buys.' And then I hand her a basic decision-making book.

"If she's mature enough to look down the road, she may decide to consider adoption for her child. She may figure this could be a beautiful thing for her child as well as herself."

Mindy Plans an Adoption

As her father and I talked, Mindy sat on the couch hugging her pink teddy bear with the red ribbon around its neck. She looked young and vulnerable, a small 17-year-old frustrated because she still weighs 123 pounds. She started out at 95 before she became pregnant. She doesn't look overweight now, but can't get back into her size 1 clothes, she says.

Russ, with an occasional comment from Mindy, talked about making the decision and choosing the adoptive family:

Russ: I knew early on that adoption would be best. My wife is an invalid and couldn't have helped Mindy. I checked on daycare and learned how expensive it is, and how scarce it is for infants. Mindy wanted to take care of her baby, but she also knew she'd have to work.

Toward the end, Mindy got a lot of flack from her friends. They were telling her she was making the worst possible decision. What kind of mother would do that?

I told Mindy that if anyone told her adoption was a terrible thing to do, to talk to somebody who would discuss both sides. I told her to talk about it with her counselor.

Talking with her friends would give her one side – that she should keep her baby – and talking with the adoptive parents (she had already selected them) would give her the other side. She didn't need to be pushed either way. She had to make her own decision.

The counseling she got from the adoption center was invaluable.

I think she probably listened to me more than anyone else. At one point I said, "We're back to where we started. If you keep the baby, we'll support you as much as we can. If you release, we'll support you. It's your decision."

Since she released, many people have said they wished we had let them know because they would have loved to adopt Mindy's baby, or they knew someone who wanted a baby. But I think we did it the right way. The counseling she got from the adoption center was invaluable.

Mindy talked several times with the counselor before she ever looked at any of the files of adoptive parents. Then she asked me to go with her, and we looked at several resumes. Mindy asked my opinion, but it was important for her to do the choosing.

We wanted somebody with enough money to be able to afford a court battle if Lee (birthfather) were to sue for custody. At one point he threatened to do that.

We wanted somebody who didn't have other children, and the couple she chose had been trying for eight years to have a baby.

We wanted someone who would be home taking care of the baby instead of working. Peggy (the adoptive mother) had already made that decision. She was quitting her job at that time whether or not Mindy chose them. We wanted somebody with lots of children around, and they have nine nieces and nephews.

Mindy: They were willing to take a handicapped child.

Russ: We liked that. So many people say if it's not pink and perfect they don't want it.

Mindy: Also they had been married for awhile, but they were still young enough, not too young or too old.

Once you get yourself into this situation,
you can't be a kid any longer.

Russ: Their faith was very strong which was a positive note for me and for Mindy.

Mindy: The open adoption made the entire difference. If I never saw her again it would be harder. I get letters, cards, pictures. The old adoption – I could never have done that and not know where she is. I would be raising her now which wouldn't have been a bad thing. I love her very much but I feel they can give her so much more than I can, and they're more ready.

I feel you have to be emotionally ready to raise a child, and I don't think I am. I've seen a lot of teenage girls out there struggling to raise their babies. And I've seen the kid's situation going back and forth between Mommy and Daddy and the parents constantly fighting.

Russ: I suggested to Mindy that she write down everything she could think of about keeping and releasing the baby. She did the same thing about Lee keeping the baby.

Mindy: Dad told me to read and to talk to people. It might help some of the girls who are considering adoption to talk to someone who has been through it.

Once you get yourself into this situation, you can't be a kid any longer.

6

HANDLING THE HOSPITAL STAY

The most carefully made adoption plan may seem impossible to the grandparents as they see their grandchild for the first time. It's important to remember that parents' support for the birthparents' decision – whether that decision is to release their baby for adoption or to keep – is even more vital at this time.

*Val, who works in a hospital, discussed the pain she sees after delivery, the pain caused by parents who either tell their daughter she must place her child for adoption **or** she must keep her baby to rear herself:*

I'll never understand parents who don't back their daughter up when she's releasing. Neither can I understand those who say she *must* release. Neither gives her a choice.

We had a teenage patient who wanted to keep her baby, and her parents said, "No, absolutely not." It breaks my heart because I know if my daughter had come to me and said, "I want to keep my baby," I'd have said, "Fine, we'll

make the best of it." I told Rhonda up to the day she went
to the hospital that she could change her mind, but she
said, "No, this is the best way to go."

*Other grandparents are more subtle with their pressure,
according to Sharon Kaplan, Parenting Resources. She reported
one grandmother telling her daughter in the labor room, "Just
in case you change your mind, I have a car seat, bottles and
clothes in the trunk."*

*"These subtle mixed messages can confuse the daylights out
of the young woman," Kaplan wryly observes. "It's as if the
parent is saying, 'Oh, gosh, are you sure you really want to
do this?'"*

*"The birthmother needs support from her parents more than
ever when she's in the hospital," observes Jennifer Stebbins,
Christian Adoption and Family Services, Anaheim, California.
"Parents need to keep outside pressures away, and they also
need to be consistent with what they've said before she delivered," Stebbins continues. "If the parents say something different in the hospital than what they've been saying at home, it
confuses her.*

*"I tell them the first time I talk with them that they're going to
be surprised at the feelings that surface when this grandchild is
born. The intensity of those feelings will surprise them,"
Stebbins says.*

Joan, 13, Says Goodbye

*Joan was only 13 when her baby was born. It was an ex-
tremely difficult time for Joan and for her mother, Anne, who
shared their experience:*

We'd gone in for Joan's checkup, and the doctor said
the baby was coming soon. I went out and told her,
"You're going to have the baby today."

I took her to the hospital immediately. By the time we
got there she was feeling the contractions, but they weren't
painful yet.

Joan's father had been called. He and his wife were

Joan's father had been called. He and his wife were
there, my best friend was there, and my boyfriend
was there.

I stayed with Joan. The anesthesiologist came in and
gave her the necessary medication. He and the doctor
stayed with her until the baby was born, a little boy. We
had a direct line to the waiting room, and I called them
immediately.

I waited until I could leave Joan, then I went downstairs
and I broke down. I couldn't before that. I just collapsed.

They only kept Joan overnight. I picked her up the next
day and that was very hard, to leave the baby there. Joan
stayed in bed all day, and I took care of her.

> *"Mom, please, I want to see him
> one more time."*

The next day she begged me to take her back to the
hospital to say goodbye. I didn't think that was a good
idea. I said, "Joan, it's going to be so hard on all of us."

But she cried and said, "Mom, please, I want to see him
one more time."

She took her camera with her. The hospital was very
good. They partitioned off a place for her to sit, they had a
rocking chair, and they didn't bother us. They let her hold
him as long as she wanted to. We stayed nearly two hours.
Joan cried and cried.

I had written a letter to the adoptive parents, and I left it
at the hospital. I told them how much we loved the baby,
how much it hurt to give him up, and how we knew they
would love him and protect him. I told them if they wanted
to contact us, to please do so, that we wanted to keep in
touch if it wouldn't be too hard on them.

They wrote us a letter, and it was wonderful. I wrote to
them and sent Joan's school picture. They wrote back and
sent a picture of the baby.

Joan kept her hospital bracelet and the pictures. She put
everything in a little box, and she takes it out and looks at

never want her to feel ashamed or sorry, because she has
made a whole family very happy. I feel we made the right
decision.

She's OK, she's getting better. We don't talk about it
very much any more. The baby is three years old now, and
I know Joan's pain is still there.

Staff Support Is Needed

*Sometimes it's a hospital staff person who makes life even
more difficult for birthparents and birthgrandparents. Thila,
whose daughter, Deanne, released her baby for adoption several
years ago, told a heart-rending story about poor treatment by
the hospital staff:*

They put a "Do Not Show" sign on the baby's crib, and
they didn't want the birthfamily to be involved after she
was born. We knew if we didn't hold the baby and love her
then, we couldn't go back and do it later. This was our only
chance. It hurts, but in the long run, it's healthy.

Well, the hospital wasn't going to let us see the baby, let
alone hold her. The nurse was very rude and insensitive. It
was a nightmare. My husband told them we weren't stupid,
and we might check Deanne and the baby out and take
them both home. They finally approved, grudgingly, to let
us hold the baby.

*This kind of hospital problem is less likely to happen today
because many people agree that the birthfamily will be able to
accept the adoption with less pain if they hold and feed the baby
and have a chance to tell him goodbye. However, it's always
wise to discuss thoroughly your desires with your doctor.*

*You need to make sure the hospital knows if your daughter is
making an adoption plan. If the adoptive parents plan to be
there, let the hospital staff know ahead of time that that's all
right with your daughter. Put your wishes in writing and give a
copy to your doctor, to the head nurse, and to anyone else who's
involved with the care of your daughter and her child. The*

*involved with the care of your daughter and her child. The
birthmother has every right any other mother has until she signs
the adoption papers.*

Birthgrandfather Is Labor Coach

*Mindy's father attended prepared childbirth classes with her,
and coached her through labor and delivery. He described the
experience:*

Labor started on Monday with hard labor beginning
about 11 a.m. Tuesday. I was at a meeting, and when I got
back to my office, there was a message on the machine for
me to come home immediately.

As soon as I got there, we called the attorney's office
and the doctor, got some things together, then went down
to the library to pick up Celia who was our prepared
childbirth teacher. She had said earlier that she wanted to
go with us.

As we were flying down the freeway, a guy on a motor-
cycle came up beside us, looked in, and crossed himself.
He knew Mindy was in labor.

We got to the hospital, went into the labor room, and
they promptly tried to usher me out. "Look, I'm her father,
I'm her coach, I've seen her all her life, and I'm staying
here," I said. Mindy didn't want me to leave, and I stayed.

The hospital should have had the letter from the attorney
with Mindy's chart, but they didn't. I had brought an extra
copy just in case, and I gave that to them.

Jessica was born at 5:12 p.m., and Mindy stayed in the
hospital until Thursday.

Mindy: There was one point when I had bad back labor,
and I wanted to throw everyone out the window. But I
didn't want my dad to leave.

Lee (birthfather), his girlfriend, his mother, and a bunch
of other people came to see me at the hospital. Then the
Bartons (adoptive parents) walked in. I saw them several
times at the hospital, and we took turns holding Jessica.
Dad held Jessica a couple of times, and I took their picture.

Phil Plans Dedication Service

More and more adoption agencies are recommending a dedication ceremony at the time the baby is handed over to the adoptive couple.

Phil, who described his strong pro-adoption feelings in Chapter 3, planned a ceremony for baby Lucy. Leesa, Lucy's mother, didn't think she could handle attending the ceremony, so she stayed in her hospital room.

The ceremony was important to Phil. Two weeks before Lucy was born, he invited his family, a young pastor who is an adoptee, and two friends to attend, along with the adoptive parents. Phil's mother, Beth, described the event:

I got to the hospital chapel just before George and Lydia, the adoptive parents, came in. I had never met them although I had read their resume.

We all sat down, and Phil walked in with the baby, down the aisle to the front seat. He thanked everyone for coming and said, "I want you to know that Leesa feels she can't be here. We don't want to forget her."

Then the pastor spoke briefly about his own adoption and his joy at assisting in this placement. He read some scripture.

Phil stood up with Lucy and said, "I want all of you to have one more chance to hold Lucy." He looked back at me and said, "Mom. . ." I walked up front, and he handed Lucy to me. He threw his arms around me and hugged us both. After that, he passed Lucy to each of the others.

The pastor asked if anyone else had anything to say. There was dead silence. Finally I spoke up, "We love her so much, and we'll never forget her."

The adoptive father, with tears in his eyes and his voice breaking, said, "I want to say something but I can't."

Then Lydia looked down at her other adopted daughter who is 8, and said how much she loves her and how thrilled they are to have another daughter to love.

When Phil crossed the aisle and handed Lucy to George

and Lydia, we entered into the joy of it. I was the mother
there, and I had to set the tone. If I went to pieces. . .it was
important for George and Lydia, and for Lucy in the future,
that we be part of their joy.

We were happy for Lucy and for her family,
and we couldn't think right then
about our own pain.

We made a big fuss over them, almost as if we were
cutting off the past and our attachment to this child, as if
we, with all our hearts, were handing her over to their care.
And we were. We were happy for Lucy and for her family,
and we couldn't think right then about our own pain.

Before Lucy was born, I was close to a nervous break-
down because the pressure was unbearable. But I felt guilty
about my own pain. I had to tell myself it was all right for
me to have pain, but how can I even think about it when I
think of Phil and Leesa's experience? How can anybody
give up a baby?

We were in favor of it happening, but we felt for
Leesa's pain. I don't think she can ever know how much
we felt for her pain.

The week after Lucy was born, I got rid of some of my
grandmotherly frustrations. It'll be a long time before I
have more grandchildren, so I went into a store and bought
two pretty little dresses for Lucy. No one in that store
could know what I was going through. I was on the verge
of tears as I looked for the prettiest little dresses they had
in that store.

Phil made a mobile for Lucy's bed, and my daughter
crocheted her a little sweater. I bought an album that said
"Baby's First Pictures," and put all our pictures of her in it
for her adoptive parents. We sent all these things to the
agency, and they sent them on to George and Lydia.

Lydia wrote me a letter in which she told me all about
Lucy's adoptive grandparents. That meant a lot to me. I
treasure that letter.

Hospital Time with Baby

The hospital stay is a crucial and vulnerable time for birth-parents and for birthgrandparents. Stacy, 17, and her mother, Mary Lou, shared their experience:

Stacy: When I was in labor, Peggy (adoptive mother) came in. When I saw her, it hit me that this was it, and I almost wanted her to get out. I panicked, and I didn't want to see her.

My mom was with me when Chris was born. I couldn't believe I had created this baby. I couldn't take my eyes off her. She was so beautiful, she took my breath away.

I talked to Peggy and Ric in recovery, and they came back the next day. I let them feed Chris, and they enjoyed doing that.

Peggy brought me the photo album she had made for me. Then they told me they were leaving so I could have the rest of the time with Chris that evening.

I fed Chris every single feeding, even at 1 and 5 a.m. Every time they took her back to the nursery I could feel it, that Chris was leaving.

I thought the 10 a.m. feeding on Sunday would be my last chance, but I lucked out. By the time we went down for the dedication service, it was her feeding time again, and I got to feed her once more.

For the service, my dad's cousin read some scripture and said a prayer. He was touched by the whole thing. Chris brought a lot of people together, and I think every-body learned á little from her. It was a good experience for all of us.

Angela (adoption counselor) tries to prepare you for the worst. She warned me that the most traumatic experience I'd ever have would be that last day in the hospital. She insisted I go over the paperwork beforehand because she said I wouldn't want to do it the last day.

I thought I'd be crying, that I'd look away as I handed the baby to them, that this would be terrible. But it wasn't so terrible.

I wondered why I didn't feel worse – perhaps because I knew it was the right thing to do. Angela said later some girls are devastated while others come through fine. I didn't need to feel guilty because I had prepared myself well for that last day.

Once I made my decision, I spent the last month grieving before she was born. I did a lot of crying for that day, but I did it ahead of time. When the time came to say goodbye, I was pretty much all cried out.

I was actually happy because she was going home to be part of their family. I could see the excitement on their faces. Chris was so loved, and she touched everybody's hearts. The nurses said she was the best baby in the nursery. They told Ric and Peggy that Chris was very content.

In less than a week, I got a letter from Ric and Peggy. I felt reassured, especially when I saw the pictures of her in her new home, or rather, her only home.

Mary Lou: The doctor was protective of Stacy's interests in the hospital. The nurse who saw her through labor, delivery and recovery had been clued in and was supportive.

---

*"I want to be with her, see her
and enjoy her as much as I can
while I'm here."*

We had told them that the adoptive parents could come in to see Stacy for a few minutes during labor, but then we'd like them to leave. I was Stacy's coach, and I was in the delivery room.

The adoptive parents and their little girl were at the nursery window when they brought the baby in. They came the next day, and Stacy let them feed baby Chris once. Other than that, Stacy chose to feed Chris herself. She said, "I want to be with her, see her and enjoy her as much as I can while I'm here." You don't get a lot of time when you stay in the hospital only two days.

I'd go stand in front of the nursery window and look at that little baby – I held her right after she was born. I felt protected, somehow, that this was my grandchild and I could look at her there. I never allowed myself to become too attached to her because it might be 18 to 20 years before I would see her again.

Stacy wanted a dedication service for the two families. This occurred in the hospital chapel on the day she came home. There wasn't a dry eye for anyone, but it was very meaningful and very special.

A lot of people responded afterward when they knew what had happened. They were surprised and didn't know what to say. They expect you to be very upset, but it wasn't like that for us. I really never felt badly about it. I know Chris will be well taken care of, she'll be loved. And there's hope in my heart that some day she will choose to find out about and perhaps meet us. Even if she doesn't, she'll be in good hands.

Birthparents Take Baby Home

Until they sign the adoption papers, birthparents have all the rights other parents have. Hospital staff must allow as much contact between the birthfamily and the baby as they would between any other baby and its family. Sometimes birthparents choose to parent for a day or longer before releasing their baby to the adoptive parents.

Roseanne and Doug had met their baby's adoptive parents, Mary and Bill, before Shauna was born. Roseanne explained to Mary and Bill that she wanted two days at home wtih the baby. The Crowleys would have Shauna for the rest of her life, but her birthparents chose to care for her those two days. Alice and Tom, Roseanne's parents, described that special time:

Alice: Roseanne had the baby in August. She spent one night in the hospital, then brought Shauna home. It was actually a good time. Our friends and family who knew about her pregnancy were all here, and it was a precious time of sharing, just thanking the Lord for such a beautiful little girl. Roseanne and Doug brought Shauna home Thursday evening, and the Crowleys came Saturday.

Tom: We had her two nights.

Alice: It was a neat time for Roseanne and me. The first night we sat up until 2 or 3 in the morning just talking and looking at Shauna. That was a good time for Roseanne – she knew she would have Shauna for such a short period, and she wanted to spend all her time with her.

(Alice starts crying) I hope some day Shauna realizes all the love that surrounded her before she went to her family. We had hundreds of pictures taken plus a video so Roseanne can remember. I hope some day Shauna can see them.

The Crowleys were here, and Amy brought another young girl who had recently placed her baby for adoption. We had our house full when Mary and Bill got here.

This was the first time we had seen Bill and Mary Crowley personally. We felt such a confirmation, and they were so thrilled – Shauna was a beautiful baby. It was precious to see their faces and to see what they were feeling. Mary's mother came with them, and they stayed two or three hours.

Since Roseanne is adopted, I can relate to what they were feeling. I know I'll never forget what I felt when we adopted her. It was hard, really hard for Roseanne when the time came for the Crowleys to leave with Shauna. It was very emotional for her.

Tom: That part I remember very vividly. I could tell – it was getting late at night, they had a two-hour drive, and Roseanne just wanted to hold the baby. I had to talk with her and say, "Roseanne, the Crowleys have to leave."

Alice: *(She is crying again)* So they left, and we were all crying and trying to support Roseanne. We just held her, and she cried and cried. She cried for 10 minutes or so, but after the Crowleys got out the door, things seemed a little less tense. Everybody was still here, 15 or 20 people. That was how Roseanne wanted it. It's the way she is.

Tom: The Crowleys wanted to pick Shauna up at the hospital, but the more Roseanne thought about it, the more it rubbed against her. They thought it best if she didn't bring the baby home, that she didn't see her too much. But she thought about it a long time, then said, "I want to bring her home. I want everything to happen on my territory."

We fought it for awhile, then said, "If that's the way you want it. . . it's going to be harder, being around the baby for two or three days." We made suggestions but . . .

Looking back, I love it. I wish we could have shared that with Roseanne's birthmother. We had a closed adoption with Roseanne, and, after this experience with Shauna, my heart breaks for Roseanne's birthmother. We could have shared this sort of time.

I don't know if I could handle not knowing where Shauna is. The Crowleys are like my kids. We just sent a birthday present to Shauna. We aren't trying to undermine them. It's like they're part of our family, and it's wonderful. I wish I could share that with Roseanne's mother.

Alice: After Roseanne calmed down – and this may sound funny – she said, "I want something to eat." So we all jumped in the car and took her out to her favorite place for pizza.

The Crowleys had a lot of legal things to do. Roseanne and Doug went down to Los Angeles three or four weeks after Shauna was born and signed the final papers. They went down together, and that was a hard time.

Roseanne said Amy let them go in this little room for awhile because they knew after they signed these papers, it would all be over. Shauna would be gone. So they sat in that little room and cried together for awhile before signing the final adoption papers

Supporting the Grief Process

How do you help your daughter through her grief when you're hurting too? Sharon Kaplan, Parenting Resources, Tustin, California suggests, "It isn't so much what you say. It's

*what you do. If you have tears streaming down your face be-
cause of your own grieving, you don't have to say anything.*

"Just sit down with your daughter and put your arms around
her. Let her know you have moments like this in your life. Let
her know you're hurting too.*

"Don't hide your feelings, but do lend your maturity,"
Kaplan advises. "Don't be stoic and say, 'Everything will be OK
next week.' It probably won't be OK next week. Just say, 'It
hurts a lot today and we'll survive.'*

"If you break down and you're suffering, tell your daughter
you aren't trying to change her decision, you're just doing your
grief work."*

*Kaplan warns against keeping the birthmother so busy she
won't have time to be sad. "One of the stages of grieving is
bargaining," she points out. "'We'll take you to dinner, to a
funny movie, and maybe the pain will go away.' Actually this
merely gives her a brief respite. The pain will be back. There is
nothing you can do about her pain – and your own – except give
her hugs and kisses and help her get through it.*

"There is no road map, and each person is going to do this
differently. It may be a year or more before either of you feels a
lot better," Kaplan concludes.*

Intense Grieving for Birthgrandma

*Becky planned her baby's adoption through Parenting Re-
sources. After carefully considering her options, Becky decided
she wanted cooperative adoption. While the adoptive parents
knew they would have all the legal rights they'd have in a closed
adoption, they were willing to allow Becky and her family
continuing contact with the baby.*

*Becky's mother, Lucia, agreed completely with Becky's plan,
but she discovered somewhat to her surprise that cooperative
adoption doesn't eliminate the grieving:*

For me the grieving didn't really start until the baby was
born. Actually it started the day I went to the hospital to
bring Becky home. I was pretty much on a false high

before that. I knew the minute I woke up that day that
reality had hit, and that was it.

I wasn't expecting to go through grief. I don't know
why, but I wasn't. I had been told by the adoptive parents
that I would be Luke's grandmother, I would be in his life,
and that this would not be goodbye. I thought I'd be happy.

Because I had been told this all along, I thought, "Yes,
I'll be happy." I didn't expect to experience this grief, but
it came like a shot out of the dark. I grieved terribly. I've
shed so many tears I wouldn't think there'd be any more
left. And I didn't expect to feel that way.

I know some mothers who haven't gotten involved in
their daughter's pregnancy. They never see the child, and
they appear to be very distanced. Sometimes I wish I could
be that way.

It hurts, and I've learned it's the loss of a role. I'm the
grandmother, but it will never be the same as it would be if
Becky were raising this baby.

Even my husband – men try to be a little more detached,
but Joe grieved too. When I went to pick Becky up from
the hospital, Joe was going to stay home. I started crying
before I left. I was hysterical, and I couldn't imagine how
we could go on living after giving this baby up.

Joe went with me, and he kept saying, "Lucia, you have
to be detached. This is Becky's baby, this is not our baby.
You have to be strong." By the end of the day he wasn't
very strong either. He was going through the grieving too.

We had talked a lot about how the birth and the adoption
would take place. At first the adoptive parents were to take
the baby home from the hospital. Then Becky decided she
wanted to bring the baby home for the afternoon. She'd
have friends and neighbors over to meet the baby before he
went to the adoptive couple.

She decided to stay in the hospital one extra day, and
she had the baby in the room with her while she was there.

It's easy to be detached until you hold that baby. After I
saw him and held him, that was all I needed. I was
basically a goner at that point.

Joe and I picked them up at the hospital and brought them home, and we had a little buffet. We told the adoptive couple that Becky wanted her space that day. At some point when she felt ready, she would give them a call.

We had a good afternoon with the baby. Some of the neighbors came over and a couple of Becky's friends. We had a nice family day.

At 4 p.m. Becky said, "You can call them now." It was difficult, to say the least.

We had lots of goodies the hospital had sent home with us. When I saw Bill and Linda drive up, I ran out and said, "Put this stuff in your car now." They did.

---

*Joe brought the baby upstairs
so we could say goodbye.*

They were here two or three hours. They didn't make the first move to leave. We were all sitting on these two couches, and Becky was holding Luke. All of a sudden she handed him to my husband and said to Bill and Linda, "Go now." She went upstairs crying, and I followed her. Joe brought the baby upstairs so we could say goodbye.

At that point, they took the baby home. It was very very difficult. The doctor had prescribed mild tranquilizers which helped.

First thing the next morning I called to see how the baby was. I tried very very hard not to do that, but somehow I had to. He was fine.

The following week Becky went back to school. The very next week she wanted to take Luke to school. The adoptive mother is a dream come true. She came over carting Luke, put the car seat in Becky's car, and said, "Take him." She admits now she was a wreck, but she carried it through. Becky took him to school another day, too, before school was out. The adoptive parents came to her high school graduation and brought Luke. They're more or less incorporated into our family now, and we're incorporated into theirs.

It can be wonderful. You can have a daughter who goes through this, and you can turn it around and do the best you can. It doesn't need to be this horrible occurrence in your life, but it's still very difficult at best.

One thing I didn't realize was that it's a grieving process. Even when it's an open cooperative adoption, there's a loss, there's grieving. This baby is not being raised in our family. The legal control is all with the other family, and of course they're in charge.

It's not only the birthmother who grieves, but both Joe and I have gone through a grieving process. I'm told that it will probably take a year of grieving, just like a death.

Although I would have liked nothing more than to raise this child, I know the best thing for Luke was to be placed for adoption. That's what kills me the most – I know I'm young enough, and we could have raised him. We could have done it, but I realize my daughter is not mature enough to be a mother now. She wanted to go ahead with the goals she had. She's leaving for college in two days.

I'm having a rough week to say the least. At any rate, we felt it was the best thing for the baby to be placed in an adoptive home with a family who desperately wanted a baby. He is the total focus of their lives. I also think it's the best thing for our daughter so she can go on with her life. She can have a family when she's ready, rather than trying to parent while she's still an adolescent.

Birthgrandmother Remembers

Thila, whose grandchild was released for adoption four years ago, swears she will never forget the intensity of the grieving she experienced:

John (counselor) told me the most devastating time, the time I'd have trouble handling as the grandmother, would be the moment I first held the baby. But I found it even more devastating when I kissed the baby goodbye and they took him away. That, dear friend, was the most devastating.

7

AFTER ADOPTION – LIFE CONTINUES

Melissa signed the papers and Arnie was gone. For three months we cried and we wondered – did we do the right thing? Sometimes I wish we hadn't, that we could have raised him – and of course we could have – but we had to think of his future. Not that I think material things are so important, but the support of two parents matters to us.

After a few months, it gets a little easier to handle. It takes a lot of work to get past the grieving, and I don't think you ever really get over it. Arnie is in the back of my mind all the time, and I know Melissa thinks of him a lot. (Toni, Melissa's mother)

After the adoption takes place, grieving may be intense for the birthgrandparents as well as the birthparents, and it may continue for months, perhaps even years. People who don't acknowledge their grief may find it surfacing later.

Years ago in traditional closed adoption, the young birthmother was often told to forget her baby, to go home as if nothing had happened. Today many birthparents who released a child for adoption in the past are finally facing the grief they pushed aside so long ago. The hurt may have been compounded with the passing years, and they may need professional help in dealing with their grief.

If your daughter or your son is releasing a child for adoption, s/he may need your emotional support for months, perhaps years. At the same time, you, as the birthgrandparent, will be dealing with your own grief.

Mother/Daughter Grieve Together

Losing a baby through adoption is likely to be difficult for each member of the birthfamily. Feeling empathy for each other's needs helps. Toni continued to talk about the grieving she and Melissa experienced after Arnie was gone:

We helped each other with our grieving. I think it's not only through the pregnancy but afterward that this is important. You know you get postpartum depression. Well, you go through the stages, but there is also an emptiness there because the baby's gone. It's like a death, but it's not.

> *The idea that there is something wrong with adoption has got to change.*

We have to remember he's being well taken care of. It's a weird feeling. . .like someone else is raising him, but eventually we'll be with him. I don't feel negative about the adoption. As a single parent I really had to believe this was a good plan, or Melissa couldn't have believed it.

I was so relieved when it was over. I wanted Melissa home and her life to go on. You never think it will be your daughter, you never do.

At the maternity home, Melissa got close to one of the girls whose parents treated her pregnancy as a very hush hush thing. She had the baby, released it for adoption, then went home. She called Melissa several times because

nobody else would talk with her about her baby. She
needed to talk with somebody, and she couldn't do that
at home.

I think the idea that there is something wrong with
adoption has got to change. I'm amazed at that, having
gone through it. I was oblivious like everyone else until it
landed smack in my lap.

Melissa has a picture of Arnie, and I have another one in
my bedroom. Nobody in my family knows about him. I
always told Melissa it was a confidence, and she could talk
to them if she wanted to. So far she hasn't done that.

People come over and see Arnie's picture, but they
never say, "Who is the baby?" Nobody has ever asked. I'd
tell them. I might say "He's a baby that Melissa and I
brought into the world."

I think it had to happen this way. I really believe that
Arnie had to be born, and that he was supposed to be with
the parents he has. I think Melissa did something incredible
for them. . .what an incredible gift. I don't think there has
to be a lot of trauma behind it. I think if you're supportive,
caring and loving, it works itself out.

Birthmother Returns to School

*Stacy's baby was born a year ago in July. When she regis-
tered for her senior year, she, as the former head of the school's
cheerleading squad, found herself the center of attention:*

Today the other kids stared. "Is that her? Look, look."
Then they'd ask, "What did you have?" "Did you keep
your baby?"

I know people are going to ask questions, and I'm
prepared to tell it like it is. I know adoption was the right
decision for my baby. I'm proud of her, and I'm proud of
the family she's with.

In a way, I want to share it because there are a lot of
people who will face this situation and won't know what to
do. Many girls have an abortion. I figured I was going to
lose my baby either way, so why not decide on life?

The first two weeks of school will be hard, but I'm
ready to get back in the swing of things. I felt vulnerable
last spring walking through the hall alone. I appreciated the
friends who stuck by me.

Closed Adoption – With Contact

*More and more often today, birthparents, birthgrandparents,
and adoptive parents prefer to remain in touch after the adoption is finalized. Some form of open adoption is widely available
in many states.*

*In some areas, however, closed adoption is a more common
approach. There is no direct contact between Luanne and her
baby, but Luanne's mother, Kate, talked about their joy when
they receive a letter through the agency from the adoptive
parents:*

On Mother's Day last year Luanne got a letter and
pictures. On the outside of the envelope was written,
"Luanne, Lisa's birthmother." They're so lovely about
sharing everything.

Luanne chose her baby's adoptive family from an eight-
page description at the agency. I wish there were a way to
be a small part of Lisa's life, but the agency says that's not
the healthy way. At least the letters are helping us realize
we did the right thing.

Luanne doesn't seem to have grieved much at all, and
that concerns her dad and me. The baby is 18 months old
now. I know the day Luanne signed the papers was hard
for her. She was crying, but as far as I know, she hasn't
grieved since.

I sent a letter to the parents right after Lisa was born,
and I'm sure they're keeping it for her. Thinking about that
helps me. I told them we were deeply concerned for Lisa's
welfare, and that giving her up was an act of responsibility
and loving concern, not a giving away. I think some day
they'll let her contact us.

I'm going to write the adoptive parents another letter
and thank them for sharing in detail with us. I'll tell them

how loving I think they are for doing that, and how much it
means to us as grandparents as well as to Luanne.

I think writing this letter will help them know we're still
out here and we still think about Lisa. Somehow that helps.

Time Lessens the Pain

*Anne didn't know Joan was pregnant until six weeks before
Alan was born. She talked about the trauma of those six weeks,
and of the grieving she and Joan experienced after Alan was
released to his adoptive parents. Anne continued:*

Joan is doing fine now. But there was a stigma attached
to her for a year or so, I think because we live in a small
community. While she had girlfriends and other friends
who were male, she didn't have a boyfriend for a long
time, and she cried about that.

She felt she had been branded. Then a year ago, more
than a year after Alan was born, Joan met a boy, someone
she could talk to on the phone, go to movies, and do the
other things teenagers do.

When she decided she really liked him, she talked to me
about whether she should tell him about Alan. "I think he
has a right to know about the baby," she said.

She finally told him and discovered he already knew.
His parents also knew. He's a good kid, and I like him a
lot. They've been seeing each other for about a year, and
they're very close.

That's a difficult thing to deal with, getting back into the
mainstream. There were a lot of girls, not friends of hers,
who made nasty remarks when she went back to school.
She came home in tears several times. When I'd pick her
up after school those first months, I could tell whether
she'd had a good day or a bad day. And there were lots of
bad days.

Joan gave me the most beautiful card three weeks after
Alan was born and everything had calmed down a bit. She
told me how much it meant to her that I had stuck by her,
and how much she loved me. I'll keep that card forever.

The adoptive couple had been married for seven years and had been trying desperately to have a child. They wrote to us and told us how happy we had made their whole family through our sacrifice. That made me feel a little better – that a whole family had been given so much joy. But it's still hard.

I have to love
this one in secret.

I hope Alan will always know how much he has been loved, how often we think of him now, and always will think of him. He's my grandchild, my first grandchild. I hope I'll have others in the future with whom I can share my life. I have to love this one in secret.

I never told my parents. To this day they don't know, and to this day that bothers me. They had a lot of other problems, and I didn't feel this was something I wanted to burden them with. I'd love to tell them, but I can't. I feel I'm cheating them, but I just can't.

They're such good people, they're the best people on the face of the earth. It isn't that I think they would think less of Joan if they knew, but it would hurt them so much. I'll never know if I made the right decision. I've always thought sometime they'd find out, but they haven't yet.

My parents came out once while Joan was pregnant, and I told her to stay in bed. I told them she didn't feel good.

Joan's birthday was only three weeks after the baby was born. We all went out to dinner that night, and Mother and Dad didn't notice anything then. My niece knows, my brother knows, but they promised they would never say anything.

I have Alan's birth certificate and the hospital records. Joan and I have made it very clear to the adoptive parents that if Alan, as he grows up, wants to see Joan, to please contact us.

I know what my niece and nephew have gone through wanting to see their birthmother. I want Alan to know that even though Joan getting pregnant was a mistake, giving him to this family was done out of love. I want him to know how hard it was to make that decision.

I think the most important message is to give your child the support she needs, and never to condemn her. She needs to know how much she is loved. Even though she made a mistake, you'll never condemn her.

Early Visits to Be Discontinued

In **Open Adoption: A Caring Option** *(Morning Glory Press), birthparents and adoptive parents talk about their experiences in meeting each other and in continuing contact with each other after the adoption is finalized.*

In many cases, the birthparent(s) felt early contact with the baby was extremely important. Once the birthparents were assured the baby was getting lots of love and care, however, their need for contact tended to be reduced.

Bonnie Adkins-DeJong, Bethany Christian Services, Bellflower, California, says her clients need letters and pictures desperately during much of the first year. Then their grieving seems to lessen, she says, and they go on with their lives, knowing their baby is having a good life too.

Stacy and her baby's adoptive parents agreed to have some contact after the adoption was final. They've seen each other several times, but Stacy, almost a year after Chris' birth, has decided it might be confusing for baby Chris to continue the visits. Stacy's mother explains:

Mary Lou: Stacy graduated from high school in June. She and Ed saw Chris in February, and we might see her in July at her first birthday. I think Stacy has decided that's probably the last time she'll see her, that it might be better for everyone if Chris has a normal family life. It might make Ric and Peggy feel better too.

At some point, if Chris decides to contact Stacy, that would be fine. If she doesn't, that will be okay too. I think Stacy feels consideration for the family. She also knows she's going to have a good life herself.

I never allowed myself to become emotionally attached. A lot of women would say, "How could you possibly not?" But I think I built that mechanism into myself, not getting too attached.

I looked at the overall picture and realized this was not the time, and didn't allow myself to become emotionally involved. I think I did most of my grieving during the pregnancy.

Ted at times wonders what's going on with Chris. I think for him it's more a wondering, and I don't think he lets it prey on his mind. The only time it comes up is when we see Chris.

Stacy is enrolling in the local community college this fall to study Early Child Development. She plans to be a preschool teacher. She talked about her two visits with Chris:

I looked forward to seeing Chris, and it was wonderful to see that she was OK and how happy everybody was. The next day I wasn't regretting the adoption, but I felt kind of sad. I missed her. I wondered what it would be like if she were here. But I accepted it.

We won't see her again except at her first birthday. Even if Ric and Peggy think it's OK, I'm afraid seeing me might be confusing for Chris. She's going to be OK, and I'm feeling good

Counseling the Birthfamily

If the birthmother leaves home during her pregnancy, then returns after her child is born, she and her family may want and need continued counseling. Too often in such a situation, both the young mother and her parents expect life to go on as if the pregnancy had never occurred. This isn't the way it works for most birthfamilies.

Yvonne's parents insisted that Yvonne stay with friends in another state during her pregnancy. Her mother, Donna, talked about the family adjusting to Yvonne's return after Leanne was born:

After Yvonne came back, we as a family began to see a counselor. Yvonne had seen this counselor a couple of times before she left, but at that time her frame of mind made it difficult for all of us. When she returned, we saw the counselor together for six weeks. That helped a lot because he was very supportive and complimented us as a family. That was reassuring, to know that we're okay, that we're on the right track.

I can't say I've had much grieving, perhaps because I worked it out ahead of time. I had to remove myself and let Yvonne work it out.

Most of our friends and family don't know about Yvonne's pregnancy. She's shared it with one girl here in church. Several months after Leanne was born, Yvonne started dating our pastor's son, a young man she'd dated when she was a freshman. He knows. She shared with him right at the beginning. I think they are the only people who know about Leanne.

After Cooperative Adoption

Lucia shares in Chapter 6 the grieving she experienced after her daughter's baby was released through a cooperative adoption plan. Lucia describes the process of working out this special kind of adoption and the benefits she sees in such an arrangement:

Becky had a pretty good summer after Luke was born. She went out with her friends a lot. I think she was trying to keep busy. She's had some bad days, and there are periods when she wants to see Luke a lot. The last few weeks she seems to be detaching herself somewhat.

The finality of signing the adoption papers was hard. She delayed it for six weeks. This is a cooperative adoption, and we were planning to have the baby for two days the following week. Becky said, "If I sign those papers, Linda could refuse to let us have Luke next week."

"Those two days aren't the question," I answered. "It's the rest of his life. She could shut us out forever. You have

to have faith they won't change. They aren't going to do
that. They have no reason to do that. You have to have
faith that you'll continue to see Luke." She signed the
papers and it's working out well.

If somebody had told me last July that I would be a
grandmother, and that I would be participating in an open
adoption, I would have thought they were crazy. Now I
think it's great. I'm very thankful for a situation which
seemed hopeless at first. I thought I'd be a grandmother
and perhaps never see my grandchild. Now I have a grandchild who knows I'm his grandmother, and I'm part of
his life.

I'll be honest with you. At this point I'm not 100 percent
convinced cooperative adoption will always work. I'm
trying to have a lot of faith. I think probably that's the key
word in an open cooperative adoption. Everybody concerned in the open adoption triangle has to have faith that
the others will do what they say they will.

In our legal system now there is no such thing as a
cooperative adoption. We'll see the legal system change
sometime, but so far it hasn't. It's a relationship that's
totally based on trust and nothing else, and it's still
an adoption.

Because we're very new into this adoption, I'm filled
with a lot of hope and trying to have a lot of faith. Time
will tell. We have to wait, see what will happen, and hope
it was the right decision.

I think it is the right decision for our grandchild, for our
daughter, and certainly for the adoptive couple who adore
this baby. I'm hoping that we can all live with this
decision, especially Becky. I don't know how she'll feel
four or five years down the line when she has her college
degree, meets the boy of her dreams, gets married, looks at
this five-year-old boy, and then it's too late. I don't know
what will happen then.

From what I've heard, a birthmother never forgets that
child. Becky will be able to have constant contact with her
child as he grows up. Because cooperative adoption is so

new, there aren't enough families with older children to let
us know what may happen down the road, but it all makes
good sense.

I think we're going to see more and more open adoptions because more and more girls are becoming educated
about their rights. There are not many babies out there and,
whether wrong or right, I think adoptive parents will go
along with it because they want a baby. In our case, the
father is a psychologist and the mother works in a child
guidance center, and they both opted for this kind of
adoption.

They think it's better for the baby to know from day one
that he is adopted, to know who his birthfamily is, and to
bring us into their lives.

The way they put it is, they have adopted not only a
baby, but a whole family. They feel they have enough love,
and that Luke will only benefit from having all this love
from both our families.

That still surprises me to be honest with you. Everyone
asks me why the adoptive parents are allowing this complete openness. I think they realize there is more to be
feared with secrets than there is with openness.

> *When your emotions are high,*
> *things don't look clear at all.*

But there is nothing easy about any of this. One thing I
learned is what seems intellectually to make sense before
the baby is born may look different after delivery. Somehow when your emotions are high, things don't look clear
at all.

Two months after Luke was born, I had a very bad day.
I called a woman whose daughter is involved in a cooperative adoption. The birthgrandmother sees her grandchild
fairly often. It's working out well for them, but she told me
it's a lot of hard work for everyone involved.

"It's almost like a courting relationship," she said.
"You're going to be wooing each other. It's like family,

but it's a very quick relationship. You jump into this, and
you don't know each other." She told me bad days are
normal, and that I still had a long way to go in dealing with
the grieving. She said this was just the tip of the iceberg.

Talking with someone else helped me a lot. The most
comforting thing is to talk to people who have gone
through something similar, and to know you aren't alone.

*A year later Lucia reported, "Everything is great. I get to
babysit Luke one day a week, and he's gorgeous. It's worked out
fine for all of us."*

Birthgrandmother Still Grieving

*Cynthia's birthgrandson was adopted by Dee and Carl two
years ago. Cynthia still grieves the loss of her first grandchild.
It's not an open adoption although Cynthia saw Scott after he
was born. She has written to Dee and Carl a couple of times, but
she doesn't believe they want to hear from her again. All
communication goes through the adoption agency.*

*Karen, who is attending college now, certainly has not
forgotten Scott. She knows adoption was the right decision for
her and for Scott, and her life is going well. Her mother,
Cynthia, however, continues to grieve:*

Sometimes I wish they'd let us see Scott. For his first
birthday we sent gifts, and I asked for a picture of him in
the little outfit we bought him. But they wouldn't do that.
Perhaps Dee and Carl are more leery of my requests than
they would be of Karen's because they're nearly our age.
Perhaps they view me as a threat. I don't know how it
could hurt to have more people caring but. . .

I started keeping a journal on Scott's first birthday. The
agency will keep it for him.

Sometimes I think I can understand why some people
make an effort to forget. Maybe it's easier.

Bob won't talk about it. He thinks if something has
happened that can't be helped, you don't talk about it. I see
his anger coming out at Karen, and I wonder if he's

thinking about Karen giving away our first grandchild.
He'd have liked to have kept the baby, too, but he could
see it wouldn't be the best thing. I wish he'd talk about it
more. I think it's just too hard, and he chooses not to talk.

The thing I miss the most is talking with other people in
the same position. People who haven't gone through it
can't understand, and it's hard to talk with them.

I stayed home a lot with Karen after Scott was gone. I
tried to talk with her and be supportive. We went to the
beach one day and walked for a long time, and I think we
were pretty close. She needed a lot of support then, and I'd
tell her over and over how much we love her and care
about her, that we were going to get through this. I told her
it would get easier. Then we planned a busy summer to
keep everyone occupied.

Karen is doing okay most of the time, but it's still hard
for me. I believe firmly that adoption was the best thing for
the baby and for Karen. Bob and I would have liked to
have kept Scott and raised him ourselves, but we knew that
wouldn't be best for Scott.

Adoption was the best solution,
but it's hard not having him with us.

A friend of ours, whose mother must have been very
young when he was born, was raised by his grandmother
until he was 12. He still has problems with that. I don't
think that's a healthy way to go.

We asked ourselves, "What is the best thing we'd want
for any baby we cared about?" We'd want a mom and dad
who would love that baby, would be there every day, and
give him everything he needs. That was not going to
happen here. Adoption was the best solution, but it's so
hard not having him with us.

Of course Karen cares about Scott, but she's going on
with her life. I'm sure that's best, and I think I should be
doing at least as well. But I'm not. I wish I could see him
once in awhile, give him things, be a small part of his life.

I wouldn't burden Karen with my feelings. I don't tell
her that I miss Scott terribly. I still talk to the agency
counselor occasionally, and she tries to help me.

*Cynthia's counselor commented, "Cynthia is still struggling.
She has done no closing whatsoever. For her, the next 20 years
has this huge void with nothing to fill it. For her, open adoption
might have been great, but our agency still doesn't think that's
best for the birthparents. They usually meet the adoptive parents, and we encourage exchange of letters and photos, but we
find after the first year, the birthparents tend to get on with their
own lives. And I think that's healthy."*

*Birthgrandparents' need for openness in adoption often
surfaces later, according to Janet Cravens, Lutheran Social
Service of Texas. "Generally they haven't had much, if any
counseling, and their needs seem to surface a year or two later
with a timid phone call, 'How is the baby doing?'" she reports.*

*"The adoptive parents tend to feel more threatened with the
grandparents than with the birthparents," Cravens
continued."Perhaps it's because it wasn't discussed earlier. I
think this is the tip of the iceberg. I suspect there is this huge
group of aching birthgrandparents who aren't making that
phone call." Cravens points out that interests of birthgrandparents are less clear than the interests of birthparents, and the
birthgrandparents' pain may be less direct.*

Birthmother Is Doing Well

*Roseanne, who released her daughter for adoption two
years ago, had good support from her parents throughout her
pregnancy and afterward. Today Roseanne's life is going well.
She has completed a year of college, and she'll be married
next month.*

*Grieving is probably an almost universal aftermath of losing
a child through adoption. However, Roseanne puts it in
perspective as she recalls her experience:*

Sometimes I feel bad because I don't think about my
baby all the time. I think I must be an awful mother. I don't
cry a lot. I feel comfortable about the situation, and I don't

worry about her. If you know you did the right thing, the
baby has the best care, you don't worry about her.

People say, "I don't know how I could give my baby up
after carrying it for nine months." Well, when you think
about it, nine months out of your entire life is nothing.

I talked with one girl who, three months after her baby
was placed, went back to the adoptive parents and got him.
Then she and the father got married. They split up, and
now they're back together. Their little boy has spent most
of his life being raised by his grandparents.

---

*Stability when you're little
is what makes you stable when you're older.*

You can't just think about what you're feeling now. You
have to think about your baby's future. A lot of that
situation was the grandparents. They wanted that baby
back. And now the grandmother says at this point they
would never let him go. Looking back, however, she
knows this child would have been better off staying with
the adoptive family because he wouldn't have had to put
up with all these splits of his parents.

To me, that's the whole thing. So many times I think we
get wrapped up in "This doesn't feel good right now." That
doesn't mean it's wrong.

Maybe I look at it differently because I'm adopted. I
know a lot of adopted kids, and it's amazing how well they
fit in with their families. That may be why my parents
accepted adoption for my baby – they've been on the
receiving end of adoption. They know how they felt.

The most important thing when you're grieving is
family support. My parents didn't pressure me into my decision. Shauna would have been smothered in love if we
had kept her, but she needed a complete family right then.

When I had Shauna, people said my parents *made* me
give her up for adoption. That's baloney. Your parents
can't make you do anything with that child. My parents
didn't sign anything. It was me.

That really pulled our family together, because we all
went through it. My mom and dad said they thought
adoption would be best since I was single and so young –
and they assured me a baby isn't a good reason to get
married. I knew all this.

Then they said, "If you don't think adoption is right for
you, we'll support you in whatever decision you make. The
family is behind you."

That meant a lot to me.

*Roseanne expresses well the important role parents play in
dealing with their daughter's too-early pregnancy. She understands how difficult her pregnancy was for her parents as well
as herself. They were there when she needed them, and she
appreciates that fact.*

Parents' Support Is Crucial

*Four years after she placed her baby for adoption, Joyce
talked about the importance of her parents' support during that
difficult time:*

Now, four years later, I know I didn't make a mistake. I
gave life to someone who wanted it. People have said to
me, "I couldn't give my baby up. I'd feel guilty." Well, I
would feel guilty if I hadn't given her up. My mother
would be raising her because I have to work – and I don't
want a child who sees me only an hour each night, and
who thinks she's my mother's daughter!

It must have been difficult for my mother. The day after
the baby was born Mom stayed with me. She held the
baby, and I know it was hard for her – she has five kids,
and this was her first grandchild. However, she never told
me what I should do – she left it all up to me.

Holding her in my arms in the hospital was the hardest
part of making that decision. I just looked at her and told
her it was for her I was doing this. I know I could have
been a good mother, but I couldn't give her the home I
wanted for her.

I have a friend who had a son when she was 16. She
thought about adoption, but her mother was horrified.
"You can't give up our baby," she said.

So my friend now has a three-year-old son. At 19, she's
tied down to a full-time job, a job she hates. She's given up
(at 19!) most of the dreams she had for her life.

An Adoption Decision –
Looking Back

*Jodie's mother stressed that whatever decision Jodie made
was the "right one." She would help her cope, but she wouldn't
be a live-in babysitter.*

My mother thought I'd keep my baby. She assured me,
however, that she would support whatever decision I made.
About a month before my baby was born, I decided to
relinquish. I didn't think I even wanted to see my baby.

He was born December 23, and I couldn't reach my
adoption worker before I went home on Christmas Day. I
didn't want to leave my baby in the hospital alone so I took
him home with me.

Mom had been surprised when I decided on adoption,
but she'd always been supportive. Then she helped me take
care of him those two days at home. I hadn't talked to the
social worker when Mom left for work two days after
Christmas.

When she came home and found the baby gone, she
said, "I didn't think you could do it." It was an accepting
comment. It really was my decision.

Two years later Jodie commented:

I look at my life now and I think how different it could
have been. I have several friends who are single mothers.
One is still living at home with her mother.

"She has to work, so her mother quit her job to take care
of the baby. There is constant conflict between them. Their

ideas about discipline are very different, and they're
always disagreeing on how to raise that child.

"I think of where I would be if I had kept him. Last year
I worked fourteen days straight before Christmas. There
would have been no possible way for me to celebrate my
son's birthday with him.

I'm still active in my church. I'm leading a youth group
and singing in the choir, and I've taken several trips with
these groups. I think I'm more capable of serving the Lord
now than I would be as a single parent.

I wonder if I'd resent my baby if I'd kept him. Would I
sometimes be ashamed to say, "This is my child," just as
sometimes now I'm ashamed to say I was a teen mother?

One woman at church tried especially hard to talk me
into keeping my child. She was dead set against adoption,
and she made that perfectly clear to me.

The other day she came up to me, put her arm around
me, and said, "You know, I realize now how right you
were in your decision to give up your baby. I look at my
life – I married because I was pregnant. I see where I am
now, how my life is going. Then I look at yours, and I
think how my life could have been. I'm sorry I tried to talk
you out of it."

I hugged her.

Stacy Writes a Letter

*Stacy talks in chapter 4 about moving from no consideration
of adoption for her baby to deciding on an adoption plan, then
choosing her adoptive couple.*

*In Chapter 5, Stacy shares her experiences in the hospital in-
cluding a description of the dedication service in which she
released Chris to her new family. In this chapter, she describes
briefly her feelings as she returned to her high school a few
weeks after Chris was born.*

*While Stacy was pregnant, her counselor suggested she might
help other birthmothers by writing them a letter in which she
would share her feelings concerning her adoption decision.
Stacy wrote:*

Dear Birthmother,

To begin with, I am 17 and a birthmother who chose to relinquish her child. I've been in your shoes, and I know the heartache, emotions and confusion you must be feeling. Your biggest question probably is, "What do I do now?" Unfortunately, it's not an easy question to answer, and one neither I nor anyone else can answer for you. Only you can find the answer because it's your decision, one you'll have to live with for the rest of your life. Adoption is not for everyone, and I'm not trying to talk you into either placing or keeping your child. What I can do is share my experience with you, and hope that I can shed some light on the adoption process.

I changed my mind often. One day I would be completely sure I wanted to relinquish, the next, I would want to keep her. I was terribly confused. I felt as if I were walking in circles. I didn't want someone else raising my child, but either way, that's basically what would happen, and I saw that as a selfish reason for keeping my baby.

But what was the right thing for my baby? What would make her life happiest and most fulfilled? I put my trust in God and He put me on the right path. As time went on, I felt as though it was God's purpose for this baby to be raised and nurtured by someone other than me. It would be in her best interest for me to relinquish her.

After I selected a family for my baby, I was happy and sad at the same time. I could finally picture my baby with a family, even though I had no idea what she looked like, or even if "she" was a she. I was also sad because it was sort of final. I promised myself that once a family was involved, that was it.

Should you choose to relinquish your child, I know you will do it out of love for him or her. Should you decide to keep him or her, I only ask, for both your sakes, that you think about it seriously and completely. Look into all your options, and make some plans as to how you will support the two of you. It's a big responsibility, especially if you're young.

Either way, it's your decision, and one you will live with for the rest of your life. That's why it's so crucial that you feel it's the right one for you. Don't let others influence you. They don't have to deal with your situation, and have no idea what you're feeling or going through. But either way, I wish you luck and best wishes for both you and your child.

In spite of the emphasis in this book on birthgrandparents' feelings, it seems fitting to conclude with birthparents' comments. We must remember that the bond between mother and child is even stronger than that between grandparent and child.

The adoption triangle is a phrase used often to indicate the child, the birthparents, and the adoptive parents. Until an adoption occurs, perhaps the triangle symbol should refer to the child, the parents, and the grandparents. Just as the adoptive parents are an important corner of the adoption triangle, so are the grandparents an important corner of the decision-making triangle. The grandparents don't make the decision, but if the birthparents are very young, their parents' support is a vital part of their decision-making process.

In both triangles, the child's needs must take top priority. As Thila said in Chapter 4, "There was something in my head that said there is someone involved here who can't speak for him/herself." To keep the child within the birthfamily or release to a carefully selected adoptive family is perhaps the most serious decision with the most far-reaching effect ever to be made by a family.

Whatever your family's decision, let it be made with caring and with love.

APPENDIX

"OUR DAUGHTER IS PREGNANT!"

Six years ago Jim and Judy Glynn, Axtell, Kansas, had to face the reality of their 15-year-old daughter's pregnancy. As they worked through those difficult months, they kept a journal. They agreed to have their journal included in this book because they hope they can help other parents realize they are not alone as they face this situation. They preface their journal with the following letter:

Dear Parents,

"I think I'm pregnant." When our daughter said those words to us, the news was shattering. There are a million teenage pregnancies every year, but that's no consolation when our daughter is one of them. When it happens to us, it's a personal and family tragedy.

What is it like for us as parents? How do we recover from the initial shock, the pain of seeing our children hurt, not just our daughter, but us as a couple, as a family? How do we deal with the questions, the doubts, the decisions to be made, the support and love each member of our family needs? We pick up the pieces and go on.

Wherever you are in your journey, we want you to know you are not alone. We care about your struggle to keep trying even though it hurts because we've been through it ourselves. We think the fact you're reading this book says some good things about you, your strength and caring, respect for life, and your goodness as parents.

When this happened to us, it was a new experience we didn't know how to handle. At first we felt lost. Strange and powerful feelings affected every aspect of our lives. Our past experiences hadn't prepared us, and we had no recourse to other parents facing this situation. As we searched for ways to cope, we wondered how other parents handled it.

*In our search, we discovered there are many books written for and about the teenage mother. That's good as hers is the greatest need. One that was most helpful to our daughter and to us was **Pregnant Too Soon: Adoption Is an Option** by Jeanne Lindsay. In it we could read the personal experiences and sharings of other girls who were pregnant, those who, single or married, kept their baby, or who placed for adoption. Whatever their decision, we could relate to so much of what they were sharing.*

Family and friends supported us, and that meant a great deal, but many wouldn't talk to us about our daughter's pregnancy. Even good friends told us later they wanted to say something to us, but didn't because they didn't know what to say.

Teenage pregnancy is happening to so many, but we were the only ones we knew. Sometimes it gave us such a feeling of isolation.

We think it would have been helpful to us to have shared with someone else who had been in our situation. For this reason, we have written our experiences and invite you to read our story. In some way, we may speak to some of the feelings you are experiencing. Just finding out that other people have felt this way can help both of us to understand and accept outselves.

We don't pretend to give you advice or the support you'll receive from those who care about you, or the counseling the agency will provide your daughter and your family. We needed that kind of support, and it was invaluable to us in many ways.

But sometimes we needed someone who'd been there to listen, who could give us some idea what we might expect, someone who'd survived and could understand in a way that others can't. But there was no one like that for us. We want there to be someone for you.

We have written the daily lived experience of what it was like for us, the events, our feelings, reactions, the effect on us and on each of our three adopted children, and how we searched for ways to give our daughter the support she needed. Our choices and reactions will not necessarily be yours, and we wouldn't want them to be. You will find your own special way to make it through this difficult time. Although we are different, we share a common bond because of what's happened to us.

We hope you find the strength you need and believe in the love you have. We know there are times that are hard, when it seems our whole world is falling down around us. It was so easy to doubt ourselves, to question why we had failed to be the kind of parents and family we wanted and hoped we'd be. But we survived one of the most painful and confusing times of our lives. There was never a time when love was more needed or more difficult to give. The Lord gave us the strength we needed, and we survived and grew in strength and love. You'll make it too. We'll be with you in spirit and in our prayers.

Peace,

Judy and Jim

OUR JOURNAL

By Jim and Judy Glynn

Judy: It was Lent, and that Monday in March is a day I'll always remember, for the date is painfully burned into my memory.

Laurie, our 15-year-old daughter, called me upstairs to tuck her into bed and said she wanted to talk to me. I remember feeling warm and complimented, for it was rare for our quiet, responsible daughter to ask. However, when she said, "Mom, I'm in big trouble," my heart sank a little. But the reality never entered my mind until she said those earth-shattering words, "I think I'm pregnant."

I felt the bottom drop out and a stabbing pain and fear enveloped me. I asked her if she was sure, and her response to a few questions convinced me it must be so. I said, "Oh, Laurie, I never wanted anything like this to happen to you." I held her and we both started crying.

I asked her who the father was. She was reluctant to say, but agreed after I explained why it would be necessary. I felt a shock when I heard. I hardly knew him. Laurie said she tried to stop him but couldn't.

My heart twisted when I saw her shrink back with a reluctant fear when I told her we had to go downstairs and tell Dad. I asked her how she could have kept all this inside. I know the reason she told us when she did was that the news was breaking in the community, and at least she wanted us to hear it from her.

As I walked down the stairs, I felt numb with the pain of how much our world had changed. Was it really only minutes ago since I had walked up these same stairs? I took one look at Jim and I think he knew.

Jim: While Judy was upstairs, our 12-year-old daughter, Debbie, sat down beside me and asked if she would be an aunt if Laurie had a baby. I felt a terrible dread at the question. When Judy and Laurie came down I looked at Judy, and my greatest fears were verified. I remember sitting at the kitchen table, the three of us, and asking Laurie if she thought she loved the young man. When she said no, I felt relieved. At least we wouldn't have to deal with that problem.

> *Our whole family had been thrown into a crisis situation in an instant.*

As we talked, I reacted outwardly in a very calm manner and asked questions that hopefully would help me get some kind of grasp on this shattering news. After Laurie had gone to bed, I thought of the multitude of problems we'd face in the future. I felt weary and drained and kind of numb. At that moment, all the years of effort in trying to be a good parent seemed to have been wasted.

I knew it wasn't just a tragedy for Laurie. Our whole family had been thrown into a crisis situation in an instant. How would Judy and I be able to hold up and still be able to give Laurie the tremendous amount of support she needed? How would this affect the other kids? Where would we go to get answers for the many practical problems that would arise? So many questions, it was mind boggling, and the unknown future that loomed ahead was frightening.

Judy: We saw the doctor the next day. He confirmed what we already knew. . .Laurie was four months pregnant. The awful reality of those words. My mind was blank for I hadn't let myself think beyond finding out for sure. What did 15-year-old girls do who were pregnant? I vaguely recalled girls going away to distant cities or homes for unwed mothers. I couldn't believe that term applied to us.

Fortunately, our doctor asked us about Laurie staying home with us. Of course. It would be no time to be away from each other. We'd need to give and receive all the love possible. I couldn't yet face the idea of her getting big and pregnant. I felt sick inside at the thought, a weak shaky feeling. I didn't want us to hide, but I felt like it as I listened.

It was a scary thought to think
her choice might not be ours.

The doctor asked Laurie what her plans were for the baby. She said adoption. The baby. . .I hadn't thought that far either. How could this most special event begin with so much pain? Our three children are all adopted. Surely, I thought, being adopted herself, Laurie wouldn't consider any other choice. Still, I knew whatever happened, we needed to ask her what her choices would be and give her the support she needed. It was a scary thought to think her choice might not be ours.

Jim: For the first week, I was in a daze. I would be working, and every so often it would hit me. My God, our beautiful Laurie is pregnant. I felt desolate at these times. I was shocked and disappointed. Like any father, I wanted the best for my daughter, and she was pregnant at 15.

There was so much about the situation I didn't know and wished I did, but didn't ask. Things were tough enough now for Laurie without complicating them with more questions. She needed support, not questions or accusations. She made a mistake that would echo long into the future, but I figured being human, we all make mistakes. We as a family had to continue our life and prepare for the future. But that first week, I wasn't much help to anyone, me included.

Judy: I went back to work at the hospital the next day. One of the first things to greet me was the arrival of the first baby of

one of the nurses who works with me. I'll never forget the look
of pride and joy on the grandmother's face when she came in
that morning, beaming over her first grandchild. It was a stark
contrast to the pain I felt inside as I listened to her and thought
of my own first grandchild.

> *I felt like an actor playing a part
> while the real me was dying inside.*

The first week, nothing would erase the pain. It was present,
consuming my awareness, or was an ache in the background that
would burst into a searing pain at the slightest reminder. At
times it left me weak, and I'd have to go off by myself and take
a few minutes to recover just to go on. I felt like an actor playing
a part while the real me was dying inside.

Everything was a reminder – to see a baby or hear an adver-
tisement on TV. Everywhere we went, we saw babies and their
mothers. It was painful to see them together – the way they
should be. I imagined being present when Laurie delivered, and
crying without being able to stop. This was my first close family
experience with pregnancy, and my heart was breaking at the
thought. I was sure adoption would be Laurie's most likely
choice, and the pain of being told we could not have our own
children returned.

It was like being told twice, first to be denied the natural joy
of childbirth, and now I would lose my first grandchild as well. I
think it hurt more the second time around because I was losing a
dream of love and happiness for my children as well. It was
painful to see them hurt, and to know I hadn't been able to
prevent it. I cried for my children I love, for the children I never
had, and now for the grandchild that would never be mine to
know and love.

Jim: It seemed strange to talk of ordinary things with Laurie
the first days after she told us. I was filled with powerful feelings that were hard to talk about. I looked into the past and
wondered what we could have done to have kept this from
happening.

It explained so many things and raised so many questions. We didn't know it at the time, but Laurie's experience with this boy had happened in October. Her behavior was different and upsetting during the following weeks. We didn't know what was wrong, but we knew something was. We sought the help of a psychologist in early December. After a few visits, things seemed to be going well enough.

We found out later the psychologist never got close to the real problem, but neither did we. I never suspected. I thought about sex, but dismissed it because I thought Laurie was too mature and sensible. I did wonder why she hadn't had any dates recently, but it was just a nagging concern at the back of my mind. It didn't seem to bother Laurie so it didn't really bother me.

Judy: When Laurie told us she was pregnant, she said she had been drinking. When I asked myself how it could have happened, I thought this was a factor, plus her age and inexperience. I didn't expect her to have the courage or the skill to know how to stop him. I blamed myself for not objecting more to drinking, or for not preparing her to better handle such a situation.

---

*It seemed no part of our life
was left untouched.*

So many thoughts went through my mind. Why? How did it happen? Was she telling the truth? I remembered myself at 15, the awkwardness, my inexperience. I wouldn't have been able to handle someone who was pushy either. But Laurie seemed so much more confident and sure of herself than I had. I didn't think she'd have any trouble. Why hadn't I prepared her better? What if we'd said this, done that? Could we have prevented it?

I worried about the greater risk in pregnancy at her age and what her life would be like after the baby was born, whatever happened. At times my heart went out to her, and I wanted to hold her close. Other times I'd feel desperate, torn by doubts about myself and Laurie, resentful of the turmoil that had come to our family.

My heart twisted with pain and love when I would see the hurt in Laurie's eyes, or think of all she'd already been through and know it was just beginning for her. In many ways, I was proud of her courage in making the more difficult decision to choose life. If it wasn't easy for us, it was even more difficult for her, and had been for some time. I looked for ways to lift myself out of my own pain to see hers and let her know how much we still loved her. Indeed, the crisis helped me realize how much I did love our daughter and how precious she was to me.

The powerful feelings Jim and I were each experiencing carried over into our relationship. It seemed no part of our life was left untouched. It was hard to share what I was feeling. I was quicker to judge that Jim wouldn't understand or care. I knew I needed to be held even as I withdrew from his touch.

I watched with alarm as I saw Jim withdraw into himself as well. He looked like he had the weight of the world on his shoulders and was ready to explode. It prompted us to write our feelings down to share with each other. I wrote that it felt like a whirlwind coming at us from all directions, but even though our world was falling down around us, we still had each other. God still loved us, and would help us create good out of this impossible situation. Often those first weeks, I felt myself go up and down like a runaway roller coaster with the strongest feelings I'd ever experienced in my life.

Jim: I felt smothered by life and weighed down by the added worries and responsibilities of Laurie's pregnancy. At times I wished I could walk away from it all, shuck all the responsibilities for 30 days. It sounded refreshing and impossible. I felt explosive, as if I were walking on eggs. If I blew off steam, the rest of the family would tiptoe, and Judy was worried. If I was quiet, Judy was worried, too.

*We began to write down
the powerful feelings we were experiencing.*

Laurie seemed to be a model citizen, and it was probably a good thing. I was afraid to lash out at her. Maybe that's why the

faults of Mike and Debbie, our other two kids, were more
glaring and irritating than usual. At times I felt fed up and
harried by all the problems.

Judy and I seemed to be withdrawing from each other. I felt
burdened, but knew in my head I needed to work for a more
positive outlook. I needed to be able to respond to Laurie, and to
Judy, too, as well as the rest of the family.

Judy needed support and so did I, so why were we going it
alone when our strength lies in each other? I hated to see the
hurt and sometimes the agony in her eyes, and wished I could
wipe it all away. We began to write down the powerful feelings
we were experiencing, and had many talks together that helped
both of us even if we didn't get everything solved.

It was a Monday when Laurie told us. Mike is our 16-year-
old son and we didn't want to tell him and Debbie until we'd
seen the doctor and knew for sure. Besides, we were still in a
state of shock ourselves. We were too late though. Debbie had
already heard at school and Mike did the next day.

When he heard, Mike ran from school in tears to tear out in
his car, with his girlfriend crying and running after him to try to
stop him. Always sensitive to others' opinions, Mike was
mortified, angry, confused, devastated. He wanted to run away,
and Laurie told us later the only reason he went back to school
the next day was for her sake, so she wouldn't have to face
everyone alone.

Debbie's reaction was a lesson for all of us. With delight in
her voice, she said, "I'm going to be an aunt!" She alone was
touched by the joy of new life. I had a long walk with Debbie on
Wednesday, and we talked about what was happening. I think I
also overreacted to my feeling of failure to prepare Laurie by
trying to make sure Debbie would know what to do.

It was a confusing time for all of us. I was afraid of what
would happen, how people would react to us or our children. I
wondered how this would affect the way they felt about being
adopted, especially Mike.

I was most afraid of Mike's reaction. We could usually talk to
the girls, but it was always more difficult with Mike. I was
pretty sure, even at this point, that eventually the rest of the

family would draw strength from God and from each other, except for Mike. I knew this crisis would either help him grow more or drive him further away from all of us.

All five of us wound up crying and holding one another close.

The pain finally surfaced after supper on Friday evening of that first week. When Mike broke down and cried, Laurie, with tears running down her cheeks, said, "See what I've done!" It broke my heart to hear it, and I wanted her to know that we didn't blame her. No matter what, we had each other, and we'd stick together as a family.

All five of us wound up crying and holding one another close. It was a bittersweet moment of deep love for our family. I felt more hopeful that somehow, with God's help, we would make it through. Laurie told us much later that she knew we all really cared about her when we cried together that Friday night. It was the beginning of the healing.

I also was finding how much I loved our children as I realized how painful it was to see them hurt. It was a pain that was to return more than once. They were the times of deepest grief, when I would cry without stopping.

We had known the joy of adoption; now we were finding out what it must have been like for the families who gave us our children. We knew first hand the great joy that might come to someone if Laurie could give them her baby, but at this point, we were only aware of the pain and confusion in our life. Still, we were beginning to take our first faltering steps.

We knew the news would spread to the surrounding small communities so we made a trip to my parents to tell them before they heard it from someone else. It was with fear and dread in my heart that I thought about telling them. I could only imagine what Laurie went through when she thought about telling us. My parents had had enough heartache in their lives, and I hated to bring another burden to them.

Their reaction should not have surprised me, but it did. They didn't fall apart. The quiet strength their own crosses had given them was evident from the beginning, and was a support all through Laurie's pregnancy. In my parents I found the only people with whom I could share everything that happened to us with no reservations. They listened, questioned at times, but supported us in the decisions we made, even when they didn't understand. It was a precious gift of acceptance and support when we needed it, and I'll always feel grateful.

I kept making excuses to put off making the phone call to my brother and two sisters. When we finally did, we found acceptance and support. My older sister lives in a city quite a distance from our home. She remarked that it was too bad everyone knew because Laurie could come live with her and no one would have known. I didn't agree with that, but recall it was my initial thought too. I knew she was expressing her caring in her offer. I think there was more awkwardness from my brother and other sister, wanting to support us but not really knowing how to say it. But each of them in a letter, a call or a long walk found a way to say "I love you," and that was the message we needed.

Jim: When we told my only sister, she was very understanding. She had helped a girl who was pregnant at 17, and who kept her baby. Perhaps that enabled my sister to accept the news as part of life without falling to pieces over it. She shared the problems of boredom and depression that she had dealt with, and urged us to look for ways to keep Laurie busy during the long months of pregnancy. Her caring but practical response helped me get a better handle on the situation.

It was hard to communicate the depth of our feelings and the turmoil it was creating in our lives.

During the first few weeks there were only a few people who said anything openly to us about Laurie's pregnancy. Each of those who did had experienced pain in his/her own life in some way and was able to risk reaching out to us. They must have experienced how much it meant, and it surely was a gift we needed.

There were probably a few people who relished our plight, but most people expressed support that was silent, but nonetheless present. They'd go out of their way to talk to us at Mass, and the handshakes at the sign of peace were firmer and warmer than usual. Still, we experienced a sense of isolation from being with people who cared but wouldn't talk about what was happening to us.

The week after Laurie told us, we chose a couple to talk with, people who were good friends. I was vaguely uncomfortable as we were sharing with them. They were sympathetic and understanding and we knew they cared. However, it was hard to communicate the depth of our feelings and the turmoil it was creating in our lives.

Our friends listened to our story, but it was like a veteran sharing the experience of battle with one who hadn't been there. Still, they gave us the gift of caring and an early awareness and appreciation for the gift of new life, whatever the circumstances. Our friends had lost four children in miscarriages and a stillbirth, and they helped us realize early that there was a new life to care about above all.

The baby was real to me from the beginning, my first grandchild, precious and beautiful.

Judy: The first few weeks I felt like a bug under a microscope. Whether we were or not, I had the feeling we were being stared at and talked about wherever we went. I felt self-conscious for us and for Laurie, but I wasn't about to hide, and I didn't want her to either. I'd had enough pain in my life to know that no matter what happens, the sun still comes up the next morning and life goes on. If we could meet adversity square in the face and still survive, maybe even grow from it, we would become better and stronger people.

I wanted that for Laurie, and yet. . .I'd see other young girls her age and wonder why it had to happen to her. A tender sad regret would fill me that she had to go through all this, especially at her age. It was times like this that miscarriage would cross my mind, and I'd think wistfully that it looked almost appealing. I wanted to pray for a miscarriage, except at the same time I wanted the baby to live.

I could see why so many would choose abortion. It looked like an easy solution. For us, everyone knew anyway, but it surely would have saved Laurie and all of us from going through all that loomed ahead. It looked like a monumental mountain, and we were just beginning. But abortion was never a choice I'd want us to make, no matter how difficult it would be. I knew Laurie could have chosen that road, and we might never have known. I was grateful and proud that she had made the more difficult choice, to let her baby live.

The baby was real to me from the beginning, my first grand-child, precious and beautiful. Whatever was happening to us, I could separate the baby in my mind and heart from the tragic circumstances.

I knew I wanted to see this new creation and hold him or her in my arms. Somehow it was a comforting and painful thought all at the same time. There was tenderness and grief in my heart whenever I thought of the baby, and a wistful sad longing that it could have been different.

Our children had perhaps come from a situation like ours. I remembered how much that same ache and longing to have a child can be present, and what this baby would mean to someone out there if that were Laurie's choice. It didn't lessen the pain, but it gave it meaning.

Jim: As Laurie grew bigger, it was quite obvious she had another life growing inside of her. I didn't resent the baby because it was blameless, but when I'd see or think of a baby, my mind raced in a lot of directions. It was an old-fashioned idea of mine that if someone got a girl pregnant before they were married, I wouldn't expect the girl's father to accept that baby as his grandchild. I didn't either, and to me, the baby was just an "it." But my thoughts were all jumbled up, and my feelings were ever-changing.

Judy: For her sake and the baby's, Jim and I agreed we hoped Laurie would be able to go through with her initial decision to adopt. However, our feelings and the way we looked at the baby were so different. It was a difficult area for us to discuss. It was hard for each of us to understand and to listen to what the other was saying.

Jim had such iron control of his feelings that I was afraid he would close himself off from becoming emotionally involved. I didn't want to lose our first grandchild and grieve by myself. I didn't expect him to feel the way I did, but I hoped he would grow to care enough about the baby to cry with me and not just watch me cry. I wanted us to give away our baby with love, and it was depressing to hear the coldness that would come in Jim's voice when he spoke of "it."

Jim: Within those first weeks we recovered enough from the initial shock to try to put some order in our lives and do what needed to be done. I had never been around anyone who was pregnant, and I didn't know much. I felt strange. I always presumed my kids would marry and, in time, call me on the phone and tell me I was a grandpa.

> *We were looking for help*
> *any place we could find it.*

All at once I was closely involved in a pregnancy, and I needed to get informed in a hurry about a lot of things. We all were reading prenatal care books. Our clinic had none written especially for single or teenage mothers, and the continual references to husband and wife were painful. This constantly reminded us of the way it should be, the way the birth experience was not to be for us.

We talked to the school about how to cover classes for September when the baby was due. We contacted the adoption agency and set up an appointment. For sentimental reasons Laurie wanted to return to the agency where we had adopted our kids. We didn't know where we'd find practical things like maternity clothes. We called Birthright for information and set up a time to find out what help was available. It was all strange and new, and we were looking for help any place we could find it.

Judy: Laurie wanted to deliver at the hospital where I worked. I knew in some ways that would be harder, but I didn't want her to go to some strange place. Her health and the baby's were most important, and we knew and trusted the doctors and staff at our hospital. Especially good was the young physician's assistant who primarily cared for Laurie. His gentle and kind acceptance of her was a most positive influence on Laurie.

Still, when I thought of telling the people I worked with or imagined us going through labor and delivery, I was dying inside. At the same time I was glad they were there.

I was used to dealing with people from a position of strength, confidence or service. It was uncomfortable and embarrassing, and there were moments when it was scary and humiliating to be so vulnerable, and to be the one who needed help. In most cases the feelings would pass in the presence of kind and understanding people who cared. It was a humbling and rewarding experience.

The feelings of isolation would increase when people would avoid the obvious subject of Laurie's pregnancy. We'd talk about everything but that. We isolated ourselves whenever we played the game, too. I was almost glad that everyone in our community knew from the start. We didn't have to wonder who knew and who didn't, a feeling I experienced at the hospital because I told only a few people there.

It seemed we were in a world by ourselves,
the only ones with a pregnant daughter.

Later I wanted the hospital staff to know, but found it hard to find a way to tell them. Eventually, after the baby was born, we learned that if we talked about it, other people could too. Even good friends told us later how much they wanted to say something, but they didn't know what to say. They were afraid they'd say the wrong thing, or bring up Laurie's pregnancy when we might not want to talk about it. Most people didn't say anything.

Sometimes it was such a lonely feeling. It seemed to us we were in a world all by ourselves, the only ones with a pregnant daughter.

Jim: Perhaps it was this isolation we experienced, the powerful feelings, or the great need for communication and understanding that led Judy and me to write. We'd choose a question and write our answers in the form of a letter to one another. It was an important way to stay in touch. Sometimes our feelings were too painful to talk about, yet we could write about them.

After a few weeks, we invited Laurie to join us in our writing, and she agreed. We made the same offer to Mike and Debbie, but they declined – except Debbie wrote a couple of times about the baby. We didn't follow any particular plan, just tried to write once a week and took turns picking a question.

Some of our questions were "How do I feel about myself. . . when I go to town. . .or church. . .about the disappointments I see in your (Laurie's) life. . .about the father. . .the baby. . . giving him away. . .keeping him. . ." It was a revelation to see the strength and goodness revealed in our daughter's letters, especially since she seldom shared much otherwise. Like me so often, what she couldn't say, she could write down. It proved to be a most special way of sharing, like having a way to share the pain, the doubts, our faith and strength, and grow more in love because of it.

Judy: The next two months for Laurie were quiet and un-eventful days at school, but with various disappointments – the silent rejection at a school dance, staying home from the rest to avoid it, not being able to sing at the spring tea at school because she couldn't fit in her dress. Laurie asked me to go to the tea. I went, but as I watched the other girls in their long dresses enjoying life the way they should be, I felt painfully depressed and alone in that crowd of people. I wondered why this had to happen to our beautiful special daughter.

My heart ached as I watched the little children steal the show as always, then run to their grandmothers' waiting arms to sit in their laps. I imagined my grandchild at age 3 or 4, and a part of me longed to keep her and ached at the thought of giving her away. I thought of the times I'd look at a baby, listen to the proud mothers and fathers and the beaming grandparents.

I sat there and hid the pain inside me as I realized all the joyful experiences that would be denied to us. I left early that day because I couldn't stand to see the reminders of what we were losing.

Jim: I thank God Laurie had the courage to keep going places when she was pregnant. I wasn't ashamed of her and didn't want her to feel that way either. I thought under the circumstances we were all doing the best we could.

Most of the time I felt comfortable having Laurie along. A few Sundays at Mass I had the feeling we were being stared at and silently judged.

Once when we went to a parish function, I could sense the tenseness in Laurie. Before we entered the hall, I stopped and asked her if she needed some time to pull herself together. She said she appreciated the offer. I told her I felt tense too, but was proud to walk beside her. I complimented her on being brave enough to be involved in a community function like that.

Mike's hurt and frustration would come rolling out in angry outbursts.

We experienced silence and isolation, but Mike bore the brunt of the wisecracks. He was the only one in the family who was teased about Laurie's pregnancy to his face.

This made it more difficult for Mike, but he made it easier for Laurie. No one dared say anything to her. Laurie told us later that Mike even went to school one day when he was sick so she wouldn't be by herself.

Mike was out of the house whenever he had the chance, and he stayed away as long as we'd tolerate it. I wished he would share his pent-up feelings, but he wouldn't. His hurt and frustration would come rolling out in angry outbursts. It looked like he couldn't stand being around any of us. He'd tell us he wasn't going to change until "that kid" was out of the house. Then he would close up again, bottle up his hurt, and refuse to talk about the storm that raged inside him. Even if we tried to reach out and share our feelings with him, he'd get up and leave. We shared our concern with our counselor and encouraged Mike to come with us, but he refused.

We gave Mike a pretty free rein, partly because it seemed to be his way of coping, and partly because we didn't know what else to do. We were busy with the demands of the pregnancy. We kept him informed of what was happening, and once in a while he'd ask a few questions. Throughout the pregnancy, however, he remained aloof and distant from all of us.

We knew we needed to create time for Debbie and we tried to do special things with her.

Judy: One of my big worries for Debbie, our 12-year-old, was how the other kids would treat her or how much she would be hurt by all that was happening. A few months after the baby was born, I sat down with her and asked her to share with me what the experience of Laurie's pregnancy was like for her.

"Most of the kids at school were quiet and seemed embarrassed to talk about Laurie's pregnancy," she said. The boys in her class were even nice to her and went out of their way to talk to her even though they didn't mention the pregnancy. "I wasn't afraid to talk about it. Sometimes I wanted to, but they wouldn't say anything," she commented. She chose a good friend and shared with her, so school went rather smoothly for her. There were only a couple of times someone actually said anything to her.

After school was out, according to Debbie, "The summer seemed long instead of fast like it usually did." Often she felt left out because of all the attention we were giving to Laurie.

For us, it was difficult to keep up with all the demands on our time – working and our usual responsibilities, plus trips to the doctor, counseling, Lamaze classes, hobbies and activities to fill the vacuum of Laurie's time. We knew we needed to create time for Debbie, and we tried to do special things with her. And then there was Mike, too.

Sometimes we felt pulled in so many directions. Debbie felt resentful at times, and I didn't blame her. Just the ordinary appointments took a great deal of time. Debbie's behavior was sometimes out of line, of course, and she would counter our scolding, "Why do you yell at me for some little thing? When

Laurie got pregnant, you never yelled at her, and that's a lot worse than this!"

Sometimes I struggled with impatience and criticized more than usual. Little things were more upsetting. I'm sure there were times I was taking it out on Debbie when I was really upset with Laurie and didn't feel free to express it to her.

Sometimes when we'd talk, Debbie would set me back with questions like, "Can I hold the baby?" or "Can we take pictures?" I had to work through my own feelings and the effect of my past training that no one saw or held a baby who was to be adopted. I felt strange, and I didn't know how to answer her.

Jim and I were seeing John, the counselor at Catholic Social Service. He advised us if we thought Debbie was mature enough, it would be okay for her to hold the baby.

When I asked Debbie why she wanted to hold the baby, she gave her usual embarrassed "I don't know." Then, with encouragement, she explained her reason: "If Laurie is a part of this family, and so is her baby, then the baby is a part of me too." I was very touched and couldn't have thought of a better reason.

To my surprise, it didn't bother Debbie to be with Laurie when she was growing bigger and bigger. In fact, she said she never thought anything about it. She said the same thing when I asked her later how she felt about her birthmother or about being adopted. She said she just felt curious and would like to find her some day to see what she looks like.

Debbie did tell us, however, that she felt "strange and weird" when we were practicing the breathing for Lamaze classes. Apparently we didn't explain or involve her enough at first, and when we went off in the other room to practice, she didn't understand what we were doing. She felt better about it when she helped practice with us a few times.

When Laurie went to the hospital to deliver, Debbie stayed with some good friends. She cried that night because, as she said, "I wanted everything to come out okay."

She was afraid Laurie would change her mind and bring the baby home. Debbie said, "I wanted her to and I didn't want her to. I thought she probably wouldn't let me hold it anyway. But even more, a lot of people would make jokes and they'd make Laurie feel uncomfortable. I was afraid it would be much

harder for her if she brought the baby home. But it still would
have been neat."

Laurie was old enough to get pregnant but not old enough to drive.

As Laurie grew larger, we became more involved with the
pregnancy. There was a lot of waiting, with growing appreciation for the gift of this baby's life, whatever the circumstances.
Most of the time it worked out that I drove Laurie to her appointments, struck by the irony that she was old enough to get
pregnant but not old enough to drive. I wouldn't have wanted
her to be alone anyway.

Waiting became a part of my life, in the doctor's office and in
the waiting room at the agency. At first I felt self-conscious and
hoped I wouldn't see anyone I knew. Gradually though, I grew
accustomed to Laurie's increasing size, and more often felt
proud to stand beside my courageous young daughter.

I remember waiting in that small room at the adoption
agency, often feeling isolated and alone, even more so when
other people were there. I wished I could think of something to
say, especially to the young girls like Laurie who were waiting
with me. But all the usual supports for opening a conversation
were gone. I felt awkward instead of confident, conscious that
whatever I said would also sound awkward and might be over-
heard as well. So I stuck my head in a book, wishing there was a
way to reach out and break the silence and isolation.

Waiting gave me time to think and was a vivid reminder of
the reality of what was happening. It was then I was likely to
experience doubts about myself and our family. Our own faults
and little failures were so much more evident. It was hard to
believe in ourselves, that we were the "good parents" we had
hoped we would be.

Even though we were working hard to support Laurie and our
family every way we could, it was easy to be discouraged and to
see ourselves as failing to be the kind of family we wanted.
Otherwise we wouldn't be here. I knew that wasn't quite true,
but my feelings and our struggles made it difficult to remember.

Actually I was grateful for this haven in the desert. We could come for the counseling Laurie needed, and we could see John for counseling. We were glad the counseling was available. I wouldn't have wanted her to go through all she did without the help she received.

The same is true for Jim and me. We appreciated the advice, counsel, comfort, and even more, the warmth of acceptance and love. It helped me to be more aware of the power of love, and the ways we were and could be giving that gift to one another. This was especially real to me when I brought my writing book and could reflect on it.

---

*Writing was a way to communicate
our powerful feelings
and the agonizing decision
of adoption or keeping the baby.*

Once when I was waiting our question happened to be, "What is your most endearing quality?" I felt peaceful as the sounds of the city drifted in through the window and I wrote what I loved best and appreciated about Jim and Laurie.

The writing was a way, too, to communicate in more depth our powerful feelings about the baby and the agonizing decision of adoption or keeping him. However, there was always only one choice I hoped Laurie would make, to give her baby to another family who had been waiting so long.

It really came home to me how much the mothers of our three children had given to us, and I appreciated their love and courage more than ever. I was finding out, day by day, just how much it had cost them to give us that gift.

My head didn't have any problem with the adoption decision, but my heart felt the pull to keep the baby with us. I imagined what it would be like to hold our first grandchild, a creation of wonder for someone else to enjoy.

Laurie's little son or daughter was a part of us, and my heart ached at the thought of losing him. I longed to hold him in my arms, close to us always. I didn't want to let him go, or to see Laurie lose her first child.

The longing is a physical ache at the pit of my stomach that still comes alive even as I write this now. I was concerned that if I felt that strongly, what must it be like for Laurie? How would she ever be able to go through with it? What effect would it have on her if she did?

Still, we knew what it meant to want to have children, and I could see we could be an instrument in God's plan to make someone else happy. I hoped we'd be able to do what was best for Laurie and her baby. It made good sense to recognize and talk about the natural feelings of desire to keep the baby. Laurie could write about it better than she could say it. Between writing, the long drives, and the long walks for exercise, we had plenty of opportunity to talk.

Whatever Laurie decided,
we would still love and accept one another.

Outside of the natural longing to keep the baby, everything in me told me the only sensible decision was adoption. We knew in our own minds it was important that Laurie face and work through her feelings about both alternatives in order to make a clear decision and be able to live with it. This was reinforced by John, but I was a bit taken back when John told us that we would need to do the same. We needed to let Laurie know it was okay with us if she brought the baby home.

That became the question for our next reflections, "How would I feel if you brought your baby home?" For me, many feelings came out as I wrote. . .my own longing to keep our grandchild, the ache I felt at the thought of giving him to someone else to love, and how that left me again on the outside of a joy I wanted to experience.

It called to mind the longing from the past to have our own children, but also the wonder I felt that, in God's plan for us, He had given us Mike, Laurie and Debbie. We had experienced that special birth of love that grows in our hearts when we adopt our children. They had grown to be a part of us, our very own.

I could honestly say I thought it would be a tragic mistake for both Laurie and her baby if she kept him. At the same time, I knew in my heart that Laurie and her child would always be welcome, and we would support her in whatever decision she made. I knew too, no matter what, her baby would grow into our hearts. Whatever Laurie's decision, her baby deserved the best chance we could give him. I hoped we as a family would be able to do that.

Writing on this question helped me to see that keeping the baby was as much a choice for Laurie as adoption. It was a choice for us as well, and it was good for all of us to know that, whatever Laurie decided, we would still love and accept one another.

I could almost see the decision weighing on Laurie, and sometimes we'd talk about it. Much of the time though, it was a struggle within herself, and we could only be there to listen when she was ready. That was okay, even as my heart ached that our daughter had to make such an agonizing decision.

I think Laurie's counselor was extremely important for her, to help her face and talk about her feelings from both sides. It was good to have someone beside ourselves to help her through this difficult time.

---

*I felt helpless having to wait silently
for Laurie to make such a major decision.*

Jim: At first I presumed there would be only one decision. Laurie would release her baby for adoption. Then John told us it was vital for Laurie to weigh thoroughly both ways, and that in the end it would be her sole decision. This was an appalling revelation to me.

It was difficult for me not to make the decision for Laurie. I have been making decisions for our family for years, and I couldn't imagine this decision that would affect us all being in the hands of a 15-year-old.

I was afraid she might make a decision based on emotion instead of common sense. It was hard not to tell her what I thought she should do. She was just halfway through high school, surely too young to take on the responsibility of raising a child.

Judy and I both work and almost have our kids raised. I had neither the time nor the desire to start over. I think a child needs a solid environment to grow up in, one that we couldn't provide, like a family with a mother and father who wanted to adopt. It looked to me that if Laurie brought her baby home, it would create an almost impossible situation for all of us.

The decision was out of my hands, and it was a scary time for me. I felt helpless having to wait silently for Laurie to make such a major decision. When I wrote about keeping the baby, I thought of all the hard work and dedication it takes, and I felt cautious and reluctant based on experience. I also knew the thrill of bringing a baby home. I was sure the baby would receive a lot of love, especially from Laurie and from all of us, even crusty old Mike.

I felt torn about it. I wanted the best for Laurie; that was of utmost importance for me, and then what was best for her baby. If she thought that was best for both of them, then they would both be welcome. I meant that statement, but I also wrote I didn't feel confident and happy about it. I had the feeling I get when storm warnings are out and everything is quiet when it shouldn't be.

Laurie's choice was adoption.

Judy: After a number of visits, Laurie's counselor asked her to make a decision before she came back for her next appointment. I'll never forget the day she made her decision. She asked me to go for a walk with her, and for once, she did most of the talking.

It was a special time to listen and share her acceptance of her baby, and her desire to do what she thought was best for her child first of all, and also what was best for her. Her choice was adoption.

I don't remember what we said. I do recall feeling relieved, but even more, a warm feeling of tenderness, proud and a little awed by the strength and goodness our daughter was revealing by her response to all her difficulties. In spite of all the ups and downs, the bonds of love were being strengthened between us.

Jim: It was freeing to have made a commitment to one choice. John reminded us of the reality that Laurie might change her mind or not be able to go through with the adoption after the baby was born. But a decision had been made that we could work at supporting. We felt we could devote our energy elsewhere.

As Laurie increased in size, I was more aware of the baby and that it was growing closer to Laurie. To me, it was just a baby. I was still an observer, and I didn't feel any particular attachment. It was like having a relative somewhere. He was a part of the family and people said good things about him, but I'd never met him. As we talked about names, I felt sort of expectant and curious, wondering if it would be a boy or a girl and what s/he would look like.

As the time grew closer, it was like the calm before the storm. We were ready to make the best of the pregnancy and prepare for labor and delivery.

Since we were the only ones with a teenage daughter who was pregnant, we asked the Lamaze instructor through our doctor's clinic to give us private sessions. We let Laurie decide if she wanted us both to be with her. I was glad when she said she did because I wanted to be there. I looked at it as a vote of confidence that she thought I could help give her support when she'd really need it.

Judy was quite capable in this area, and I realize she could have done the coaching herself, but to me, it was part of being a parent. You don't run when it gets tough. I love Laurie and wanted to be a help when it would be difficult for her.

Our Lamaze instructor's acceptance helped us see ourselves as worthwhile people.

I had talked to young fathers in the past who chose merely to be observers when their wives gave birth. I felt sorry for them in a way, and in another way, disgusted that they let their macho image deprive them of that total involvement. I never thought I would be so involved, but I was. I wanted to learn as much as possible so that I could participate and not just observe.

The Lamaze instructor agreed to give us the sessions and was quite supportive to all of us. I felt thankful for I wanted Laurie to be as prepared as possible. I knew almost nothing about labor and delivery myself, and the first time or two I felt out of place being there. I felt like an outsider intruding on the women's domain.

It was ironic being the first grandfather to take Lamaze classes from Jo, the instructor, but she made us feel welcome and comfortable. She treated Laurie with kindness and respect, and complimented us on our support. Her acceptance helped us see ourselves as worthwhile people.

The classes were a reminder to me that Laurie's delivery time was rapidly approaching. Practicing gave Laurie, Judy and me a good plan to work on together, so that when the time came, we were prepared. More than that, we could share the experience together. If I hadn't, I never would have experienced the miracle of birth with her. It's something I wouldn't have missed for the world, and something I never want to repeat.

*Sharing Lamaze classes
was a healthy response for all of us.*

Judy: Learning about labor and birth, practicing and preparing together brought home the reality of what we were about to experience. Laurie practiced faithfully even when we couldn't. I felt confident and encouraged that she would be able to handle the contractions of labor, and we would be able to help her. The moments of sadness would still come, and the dread of what might happen, but it was easy to get caught up in the spirit of closeness. We were working together and doing something positive to get ready for the big moment of birth. Sharing Lamaze classes was a healthy response for all of us.

Jim: When the long wait was over and Laurie started having labor pains, we both knew what to expect and what to do. All the months of reading books, practicing Lamaze, and getting ready were about to pay off. Judy was at work when we came to the hospital, and fortunately, the other nurse on duty was her good friend in whom she had confided all through Laurie's pregnancy. We were in good hands.

It was a day of mild contractions, and that evening the three of us took a walk outside the hospital. It was a peaceful time of closeness, but I had a sad helpless feeling too, wondering how we could all find ourselves in such a strange position.

The contractions started in earnest that night. Labor – someone surely named it right! It was the hardest work we ever did. We were so busy being coaches, we didn't have time for anything else. If Judy and I were exhausted just being helpers, imagine how Laurie felt after she finally delivered.

---

*I was holding my grandson
and he was beautiful!*

The cloud of fatigue lifted and seemed to disappear when the miracle of birth happened and Scott gave his first lusty cry. I did truly experience a miracle. All through Laurie's pregnancy, the baby was an "it" to me, and the "it" changed in an instant to the miracle that was Scott. It was a heady thrill when I first got to hold him in the delivery room. I was holding my grandson, and he was beautiful!

Judy: When Scott was born, my first thought was the thrill of seeing him alive and well. I didn't cry with pain as I thought I might. I was amazed that he was so big!

I watched our daughter hold her son in her arms, and I felt almost peaceful, a little sad, but grateful that Laurie was willing to go through all she did. She was a mother holding her son, and whatever her age or the circumstances, I felt quietly awed by the miracle of life before me. To see Scott in her arms made everything worthwhile. Laurie was okay and so was her son.

I wish it had been different for all of us, but it wasn't. We had done the best we could. For all the pain, here before us was the joy of Scott's life.

When I held Scott in my arms, I felt myself smile inside with tenderness and love. I handed him to Jim, and together we marveled at our precious and beautiful grandson. As Jim carried

Scott to the nursery, I felt proud as any grandparent must and
only a little sad and self-conscious.

We returned to the hospital that evening and the next day to
spend time with Laurie and Scott. These were such precious
moments, to delight in holding him, taking care of him, sharing
him with our family, taking pictures, welcoming him as a part of
us. It was a good time.

My fears of rejection from my co-workers were unfounded
and my faith in the basic goodness of these people was more
than justified. A few looked uncomfortable and didn't know
what to say. That's understandable, but almost everyone went
out of their way to do the little things that mean a lot, like
bringing Laurie a TV, making her a bouquet of flowers, but
especially asking us if we wanted Scott to be with us. This made
it possible for us to share him with our family.

It was a gift of acceptance and support when we needed it.
They helped us make the most of the precious little time we had
together. They brought Scott in anytime we asked. It meant so
much to us. Most families have a lifetime. . .we had one day. We
wanted him to be part of a family who loves him from the
moment of his birth, and he was. Debbie got to hold her little
nephew which was important for her. Mike didn't, and that was
okay.

My parents had shared so much with us, and it was good they
could share this time with us too. I felt a real sense of family to
see my mother holding Scott in her arms. My father didn't – I
think he was afraid he'd cry – but I've never seen him touch
anyone as tenderly as he touched Laurie on the cheek that day.

Maybe holding him stirs all the natural longings to keep him
with us. I know it was one of the fears expressed by others that
if we held him, it would hurt more, and perhaps we wouldn't be
able to go through with our decision. But the feelings, the desire
to keep him had been there for some time, whether we held him
or not. I wanted Laurie to keep him as much, perhaps more, than
I wanted her to let him go. But if she had changed her mind, I'd
want Laurie to find out then and not later.

The pain of losing someone we love would have been there
regardless, and I'm glad we could spend the time with him that
we did. The pictures, the memories are precious moments to

remember. He will always be a part of us, but now we can remember the special time we shared with him, not just the separation and loss.

Jim: I'll always remember that day. We had time to be with Laurie and to get acquainted with Scott. To me, it is one of those days when time stood still. The waiting was over, the pain was past, it was a day to rest and marvel at God's creation. Then the next day arrived, the dreaded day of relinquishment. All arrangements had been made to sign the papers. Judy and I looked at Scott one more time and went to Laurie's room. Soon it was time to sign.

Our first grandson is with a family who loves him.

I have experienced some tough situations in my time, but being present when Laurie signed away her rights to the person she loves so much was a genuinely heartbreaking time. As we waited in that hospital room those ten or fifteen minutes for Scott to leave for his new life, it seemed like a lifetime. If it was that way for me, how was it for Laurie? Laurie had the courage and good sense to do what was best for her and for Scott. At least she has the satisfaction of knowing that Scott is part of a family with a mom, a dad and a sister who love him. I'm afraid if I were Laurie, that would be small consolation.

Life can be cruel sometimes, and it takes a lot of strength and caring to live it to the fullest. As for me, I feel at peace about it now. We did a good job of supporting Laurie from start to finish. Our first grandson is with a family who loves him. I realized when Laurie signed those papers that I would never see him again, not in this life anyway. I think for now I prefer to leave it that way and look forward to the time I can.

Judy: The next day was a sad and empty day. It was hard to see the good in the choice we made. We missed Scott and wanted him back. But we knew, too, that he was safe and happy with his new family.

Mary (Laurie's counselor from the agency) called Laurie and John called us to tell us about Scott's arrival and the birth into his new family. That meant so much to all of us. It made it real that he was okay. The images of his reception and the description of the joy when his new parents held him reassured us that what we hoped for and wanted for him was really happening. It was a comforting thought.

However, in the days that followed, the heartache of losing him was much more present than that awareness. The grief would come and go, but it was there.

As time passes, we feel more and more
at peace and happy for him.

A couple months later we spent one harrowing night searching for Laurie because of that grief. She had gone out with her friend and had gotten in her car to drive home, but she didn't get here. From 2 a.m. to 4 a.m. we searched the roads and ditches, called the police when we couldn't find her, died a thousand deaths. Then she drove in our yard at 4 a.m.

As she was driving home, it hit her that Scott was gone, and she wanted him back with all her heart. She cried and cried and fell asleep. Her longing to have him back was so strong. My heart aches knowing how present the grief was for me at times and how much more it was for her. As time passes, though, we feel more and more at peace and happy for him.

Laurie has a book with his pictures, his footprints, a copy of the information about his new family, and the letter and picture his adoptive mother sent to us a few months after he was born. We don't need to do it often, but when the grief comes back, we get out his picture and remember. I can smile with the tenderness I felt when I held him, and delight in the gift he is to us as well as to his new family. Laurie says for her the book brings back good memories of the time he was with her. It's a special book for the precious memories we have for Laurie's first special son.

I'm more aware of the mothers of our children than I've ever been. I think this whole experience has brought more understanding for their own most difficult choice. It was good in the case of each of our children to again let them know what special people we think their mothers are, and how much we appreciate their gift of life and love.

I see that picture and know. . .
he's alive and growing, and he's beautiful.

Somewhere out there, someone must be saying that about our daughter, too. . .I think of our grandson with tenderness and wonder how he's growing and what he looks like. The picture his adoptive mother sent to us later is truly a gift. I can look at that picture and see for myself. . .he's alive and growing, and he's beautiful. I can see that he is loved and happy, and I feel joy that all we wanted for him is happening.

When Laurie looks at his picture, she says she feels at peace in her heart and knows she made the right decision. Jim says he'd prefer to close the door, but for me, that second picture was important, and gives me a peaceful joy. I am content to let him become and grow with his new family. I trust in their love and know they will do the best they can.

I do feel an ache in my heart when other people glow with the stories about their grandchildren or show their pictures. In a sense, we still experience the isolation of not being able to talk about the feelings we experience for our grandchild. But the ache passes. What lasts is the love we feel for Laurie in making her most difficult choice, and the love we feel for her son and his new family.

What were some of the things that helped us through Laurie's pregnancy? Even initially when it was so painful, I felt the closeness of God. He knew what each of us was going through, and as a Father who loves us, His children, I thought He must be crying with us. He didn't want to see us or our children hurt any more than we did.

Passages that had always meant a lot to me spoke to me in my grief, like Romans 8, "If God is for us, who can be against us . . .there is nothing that can separate us from His love. . ."
I believed that and I felt it that Easter. We had never

experienced a more painful Lent, and I can still remember the closeness that Jim and I felt to each other and to Jesus that Easter at Mass. We knew how much it meant that he loved us.

Being at Mass was a vulnerable time each week. It brought us face to face with our community and our God just as we were. It made me sharply aware of whatever feelings I was experiencing at the time. It confronted me with my sadness that this was happening to us when we'd sing songs like "Yahweh I know you are near, standing always by my side. You guard me from the foe. . ." I wondered why God had not guarded us from the foe who had brought so much pain and heartache into our lives. I could ask God "Why?" or "Where were you when Laurie needed you?" without really expecting an answer.

I realized from earlier painful experiences that God has not promised that only good things will happen to us in our life, but rather that He is with us in all things, no matter what happens. And He was. The love that He had given to Jim and me and to our family made it possible to believe in His love. No matter who might judge us or turn away, Jesus, the Good Shepherd, would always hold us close.

Some people were probably talking about us; most just weren't talking to us about our pain. Sometimes being at Mass made me more aware of our isolation from others. Sometimes I could feel silent support there, too.

Our parish priest was uncomfortable talking to us face to face, but he could speak his support and caring through his sermons. I'm convinced his sermon the week that Laurie made her decision to adopt was written for us. It was beautiful and gave much-needed support. We had never needed God so much in our lives, and we could be aware of His presence with us if we'd listen. We could hear Him speaking to us in His word, the songs we'd sing.

I sing and play at Mass, and when I'd stand before our community, I felt vulnerable. But more than ever the songs became a prayer for me that I could sing to our God, to Jim and to Laurie, Mike and Debbie. God was coming to us in Communion, and in the people He was sending to us in our lives. Even in the silence and the isolation, His message was and will always be, "I am with you always. . .there is nothing that can separate you from my love. . ."

Jim: One thing that helped me through Laurie's pregnancy was taking one day at a time. That was enough to handle. After awhile, I realized some good had to come out of it, but we would have to apply ourselves to help make it happen. With God's help, it was possible. Laurie's own response made a big difference. She could have let it get her down, but her courage and determination helped us as much as anything.

> *Writing helped us communicate our love*
> *and stay in touch with our feelings.*

Judy and I drew strength from the love we have for each other. Our own communication and relationship was most important. We may have felt isolated at times from others, but as long as we stayed close to each other, we were not alone. Writing helped us communicate that love and stay in touch with the feelings we experienced. Without that, we'd have been isolated from each other as well.

If we had been more open with the people we knew cared about us, we would have received more of the love and support we needed and our friends wanted to give. It's easy to see that now. Then it was hard.

The people in our lives that we did talk to were able to give us acceptance when we needed it. We've mentioned them throughout our story: our family, friends, a nurse at the hospital, the young doctor who cared for Laurie, our Lamaze instructor, the people at Birthright, Catholic Social Service, the Marriage Encounter community who started a prayer vigil when Laurie went into labor, the hospital staff. It seems God provided us with what we needed to make it through.

Judy: We weren't able to find any books that were written for parents to help us deal with this family crisis. When we visited Birthright the first time, we were given a handout, "To the Parents of an Unwed Mother." It was only a few pages long,

but how many times it would hit on target and touch some of the
feelings and the turmoil we were experiencing.

It meant a great deal to read anything that talked about what
we were going through. Somehow we were not alone, and there
was some direction on how to deal with the crisis.

Later our Lamaze instructor gave us a book list because the
clinic had no books on teenage pregnancy. One of the books we
ordered was **Pregnant Too Soon: Adoption Is an Option.** It
turned out to be most special and a helpful book for all of us. In
it we could read the experiences of girls who were pregnant as
they shared their own choices of adoption or keeping their baby.
We could read what it was like from someone else who had been
through it, and it turned out to be helpful not only to Laurie and
to us, but to our doctor and our hospital staff as well.

We'd like to share some of the areas that we had to face and
deal within ourselves. One was guilt. When Laurie was pregnant, whatever the reasons, we thought part of the reason had to
be that we had failed as parents. There must have been something we could have said or done that would have prevented it.
This burden of guilt weighed heavily on us at first.

> *We did the best we could.*
> *We survived. . .and we grew.*

What helped us was talking, writing, praying, reading about
the guilt others felt and how to deal with it, and more than
anything, talking to John at the agency. We didn't excuse
ourselves. We came to recognize and believe again that we had
done the best we could.

As John suggested to us, when our children are small, we can
usually protect them from harm. As they grow older, however,
we have to let go and pray. We did, and our daughter was hurt
deeply. But again, we did the best we could. We survived. . .and
we grew.

Blame was also involved. I blamed myself for not preparing
Laurie better. If I had warned her more, would she have been
more careful? It wasn't hard to see that blame was a trap that
would prevent us from dealing with the fact of Laurie's

pregnancy. It was a pitfall to avoid. It wouldn't change anything, it wouldn't help anyone. It was time to move on, and we did.

We had to face our doubts about ourselves and our daughter. Laurie's pregnancy shattered so many images we had of ourselves and our family.We had to create new images that incorporated this new painful experience. Sounds easy. It wasn't.

It was a struggle at times to believe in ourselves.

Our own communication was essential. If we could share the doubts and the pain, we could also share our faith, our strength and our love. It was a struggle at times to believe in ourselves.

Other people's silence and our own made it harder. Those who found a way to share their own pain or simply said, "I don't know what to say but I want you to know I care," gave us support when we needed it. New people entered our lives and did reflect our goodness and encouraged us.

Laurie herself helped by her response and in her writing when she shared what it meant to her to have us as parents. It was freeing to know it was okay and good to talk with Laurie about how her pregnancy affected us, to share the doubts and the struggle to believe in her and in ourselves again.

It meant we didn't have to pretend; we could tell it like it was for us. It was good to know the difference between feelings and decisions, that even though we felt doubt, we could decide to keep trying, to believe, to trust once again. It isn't a decision we made once, but one we continue to make many many times.

Jim: Rebuilding trust in Laurie was another task. Our trust was never really tested until after the baby was born when Laurie went out for the first time with her girlfriend. It was scary to let her go. At first we asked too many questions, partly because we didn't think we'd asked enough before, and partly because we were afraid for her and didn't want to see her hurt again. It took some time to work it out, to listen to Laurie, to realize we couldn't prevent problems now anymore than we could have then.

Basically it's up to Laurie to rebuild her life again. All we can do is be here if she needs us. That's hard to do because we'd like to protect her. Even if we could, that wouldn't be healthy for her or for us.

I feel panicky sometimes when she's late, but more and more, it's for ordinary reasons. We've shared with her what it's like for us to wait, and she has become more considerate of us and makes sure she calls.

Laurie's pregnancy now almost seems like a bad dream instead of a harsh reality. I can remember it well, but at times it seems that it never happened.

Judy: One of the crises we had to face after we came home from the hospital was Mike's behavior. We hoped it would improve but it didn't. Things couldn't go on the way they were, either for his sake or the rest of the family. There had to be a change.

After two phone conferences with John, we hammered out the limits with Laurie and Debbie, the ways we needed Mike to change, to change or to leave. Three weeks after Scott was born, we were ready to confront Mike. It was scary and we fully expected him to explode in an angry abusive outburst and storm out of the house.

I remember Jim and I lying in bed the night before, feeling heavy and discouraged about the conference the next morning. Jim's prayer was to tell God he was putting everything into His hand. . .it was too much for us. I simply asked God for a miracle.

The next day our prayers were answered! Mike didn't explode. He agreed to the limits and chose to stay. When we were through, Laurie capped it off by saying she just wanted her big brother back. He said, "I've been here all the time you were pregnant, Laurie." She told him she knew that he'd been here when she needed him, and she hugged him.

A positive effect of this experience, one that has helped Mike change, has been that Laurie has become more vocal when his selfish behavior affects her. She used to suffer in resentful silence, but now she lets him know just where he's crossed the line. It's good for both of them.

The limits are tested, of course, but Mike is changing and has become a contributing member of the family again, still immature, a constant challenge, but growing. How good it is to have him back with us.

I wonder where our family would be without the benefit of the counseling we received all the way through. There was a third party, professionally trained to listen, give advice, and help us find our own solutions. Because of it, our family was able to survive and grow. Maybe we would have anyway, but I'm glad there was help when we needed it.

Laurie says her life is changed. . . but it's not ruined.

One of the struggles we're still living with is the effect on Laurie's social life. We live in a small community, and so far no one has had the courage to ask her out. She has a girlfriend and they enjoy going out together. But when the special events come along at school (homecoming, the school dances), Laurie is reminded that no one will ask her. How long will that last? Will she ever get to experience any dating? What effect does that have on her feelings about herself?

These are my concerns. Yet when I asked Laurie about it, it's not one of hers. She enjoys going out with her friends. She knows her life has been changed and will never be the same. But as she says, her life is changed. . .it is not ruined. Her response can make the difference.

At a school dance, her friend challenged her to ask a boy to dance. Laurie said she was scared, afraid that he'd say no, but he didn't. After that, if they didn't ask her, she'd ask them. She only sat out three dances. She changed an evening of silent rejection into one of fun and acceptance.

When I first asked her, she said she didn't care if she didn't date, but later said sometimes she feels hurt. She thinks they don't ask because of what someone else might say. But she also says if she really wants a date, she can get one.

The thing that matters to me is that she feels good about herself. And she does.

The issue of birth control came up, not because either we or Laurie brought it up, but because I found a paper with the phone number of a Family Planning clinic. My initial feeling was dread at what that might mean. I had mentioned it once, but I wish I had followed up on her need to know and understand. I recognize that this is a decision each person has to make in her/his life, but it should always be an informed choice, both for understanding the methods and the church's teaching on this issue. It's a choice Laurie can make for herself whether we approve of it or not, whether we know or not.

At least I had a chance to share with her my thoughts and feelings about it. I don't think she was saying she wanted to use birth control to have sex. She was saying she didn't want to get pregnant under any circumstances and be faced with losing her child again. She wanted to know how to prevent that heartache. And that I can understand.

Jim and I believe in the goodness of sex in God's plan. We express that in the way we live out our love for each other. We have shared what sex means to us. We can only hope Laurie will choose those values for herself despite what's happened to her.

When I asked Laurie about her greatest joy and struggle, it was all centered around Scott. The joy for her is knowing he's happy and with a family who loves him, a family that she chose for him. The greatest struggle is knowing he's out there somewhere and can't be with her. She, too, is content to let him grow with his new family, and she hopes that someday he will look her up.

It's hard for us to look at ourselves,
to listen and see what we need to change.

It is a revelation to me to listen to my daughter share a strength and love much beyond her years. Her concern is not for herself but for her son. When I see the way she is able to love and give of herself and rise above such difficult circumstances, it says so much about her goodness and beauty as a person.

Jim: It was a struggle for me, especially at first, to let Laurie go out again, and all we could do was pray that she would be okay. I struggle with her quietness when she comes home and chooses either not to share her experiences with us or to share just a little bit. I look back in the past and know how her silence enabled disaster to sneak up on all of us. There's the temptation to wonder what she's not telling us, and I have that fear sometimes when she's quiet.

I feel hurt that Laurie can't quite trust enough to come to us, despite the support that we gave her when she needed it. It's a difficult area for all three of us that we're trying to work through.

It's hard to understand how difficult it must be for her to trust anyone, or to remember that it wouldn't even be healthy if she told us everything. When we asked about why it was difficult to share with us, she said because in the past when she did, we asked too many questions. It's hard for us to look at ourselves, to listen and see what we might need to change. But it's also one of the good things that's growing out of our difficulty.

Because we have a greater need for communication, Judy and I are working harder to develop better communication skills. Some of the books we've found helpful are Haim Ginott's *Between Parent and Teenager* (Avon Books, 1971) and *P.E.T. – Parent Effectiveness Training* (New American Library, 1970) by Dr. Thomas Gordon. *P.E.T.* is the most helpful because it gives practical ways to learn and use skills like active listening, the use of "I-statements," and ways to resolve conflict. We had used some of these ideas in the past but we're working harder to make them more a part of our communication.

Sometimes it's frustrating to try to change habits of years, but we can see that it is making a difference in our ability to listen effectively and communicate in our family.

> *It was a time of love when Judy and I grew closer to each other and closer to Laurie, to Mike and to Debbie.*

When Laurie first told us she was pregnant I looked at it as one big heartache, a disaster that befell her and our family, one that shook our family to the roots. Now, as a crisis that's mainly behind us, it is a happening in our lives that left its mark, a mark that will never be forgotten. It will be looked at in many ways by all of us in the future. I look back on it now as a crisis, but a time when our family held up well under fire, when all our confidence and strength was barely enough. It was a time of love when Judy and I grew closer to each other and closer to Laurie, to Mike and Debbie, a time when one of our children really needed us and we were there.

Somehow we know when the chips are down we can count on each other in our family. We don't have to wonder – we know we love each other.

ANNOTATED BIBLIOGRAPHY

One-hundred twenty-one titles in the 1987-1988 edition of *Books in Print* are listed under the subject of adoption. Mostly these are books written for professionals dealing with adoption, for adoptive parents, their adopted children, and for adult adoptees. A few books are listed for birthmothers who relinquished for adoption in the past. Even fewer are designed for young birthmothers considering an adoption plan, and none appear to be written for the families of birthparents.

Some of the following books deal with teenage pregnancy and/or adoption from the professional's viewpoint. Others are written specifically for teenagers facing early pregnancy. Not included are the many books available which focus on adoptive parents and/or adoptees.

These books for birthparents deal primarily with the dilemma of unplanned pregnancy. Some focus on decision-making generally, others on adoption specifically. Others provide guidance during pregnancy, while some stress the realities of parenting a child and/or premature marriage.

Prices, when given, are from the 1987-1988 edition of *Books in Print*. If you order a book directly from the publisher, check first with your public library or a bookstore to learn current prices. Then add $2.00 for shipping.

Aigner, Hal. *Adoption in America: Coming of Age.* 1986. Paradigm Press, 127 Greenbrae Boardwalk, Greenbrae, CA 94904. Paper, 208 pp. $8.95.

Aigner is concerned with the interests of adoptees, their birthparents, and their adoptive parents as he documents and analyzes the major challenges faced in adoption reform efforts. He also provides a fascinating and detailed look at the history of adoption in the United States.

Anderson, Carole, Lee Campbell, and Mary Anne Manning Cohen. *Choices, Chances, Changes: A Guide to Making an Informed Choice About Your Untimely Pregnancy.* 1981: CUB, Inc., P.O. Box 573, Milford, MA 01757. 63 pages. $5.00.

Book offers constructive suggestions for questions a young person should ask if she approaches an adoption agency for help. Mainly it is a reassuring booklet for young mothers who want to keep their babies to rear themselves.

Arms, Suzanne. *To Love and Let Go.* 1983: Alfred A. Knopf, New York. Hardcover, 240 pages. $14.95.

Presents the stories of several young women who release their babies for adoption and of the parents these birthmothers choose. Arms' emphasis is on the needs of the birthmothers and of the positive effects of adoptive parents and birthparents meeting and developing a relationship.

Barr, Linda, and Catherine Monserrat. *Teenage Pregnancy: A New Beginning.* Revised 1987. New Futures, Inc. Also available from Morning Glory Press, 6595 San Haroldo Way, Buena Park, CA 90620. 98 pages. Illustrated. $10. Quantity discount. Student Study Guide, $2.00

This book was written specifically for pregnant adolescents. Topics include prenatal health care, nutrition during pregnancy, fetal development, preparation for labor and delivery, decision-making, emotional effects of adolescent pregnancy, and others. The authors have obviously known, worked with, and loved many school-age parents.

Barr, Linda, and Catherine Monserrat. *Working with Childbearing Adolescents: A Guide for Use with Teenage Pregnancy, A New*

Beginning. New Futures Inc. Also available from Morning Glory Press. Revised 1986. Spiral, $12.95.

Introductory chapter presents overview of teen pregnancy and parenthood in the United States. In addition, adolescent development and sexuality are explored. Authors include their experiences, ideas, and insights gained through working with pregnant adolescents.

Brandsen, Cheryl Kreykes, M.S.W. A *Case for Adoption: A Guide to Presenting the Option of Adoption.* 1985. Bethany Christian Services, 901 Eastern N.E., Grand Rapids, MI 49503. 48 pp. $2.00

Well-written booklet designed for counselors who work with pregnant teenagers. It stresses respect and caring concern for birthparents, and does not suggest that adoption is the only option a young person could or should choose. Rather, it addresses the concerns and frustrations counselors have expressed about representing adoption as a loving, responsible, and mature choice that must be considered as seriously as parenting or marriage.

Becker, Kayla, with Connie K. Heckert. *To Keera with Love.* 1987. Sheed and Ward. Also available from Morning Glory Press, 6595 San Haroldo Way, Buena Park, CA 90620. Paper, $7.95

Dramatic first-person story of Kayla's journey from early childhood in a happy and protected home environment in Iowa to the harsh reality of becoming a mother too soon. . .and through her grieving as she places her beloved Keera for adoption. Absorbing story of one pregnant teen's decision.

Ewy, Donna and Rodger. *Teen Pregnancy: The Challenges We Faced, The Choices We Made.* 1985. New American Library. Paper, $3.95.

A refreshingly practical guide for teenagers facing the hard choices and special challenges of pregnancy in the teen years. Good advice is coupled with many quotes from pregnant and parenting teenagers.

Ginott, Haim G. *Between Parent and Teenager.* 1971. Avon Books. Paper, $3.95.

Recommended by Judy and Jim Glynn in their journal as an aid toward more effective communication within a family. It's still available and it still offers excellent guidelines for those wanting to improve their inter-family relationships.

Gordon, Dr. Thomas. *Parent Effectiveness Training.* 1971. New
American Library. Cloth, $12.95.

Also recommended by Jim and Judy Glynn. Dr. Gordon's
"I-Messages" and "No-Lose" method for resolving conflict are
classics in the childrearing literature. You can learn basic P.E.T.
theory through independent study of the book, although group
discussions in addition to reading the material would be preferable.

Hansen, Caryl. *Your Choice: A Young Woman's Guide to Making
Decisions About Unmarried Pregnancy.* 1980. 176 pp. Avon. $2.25.

A comprehensive guide to the options open to pregnant teenagers.
The author emphasizes the need for choosing an option rather than
going into motherhood without making a decision. Suggested is a
"Pregnancy Timeline" to be used in decision-making.

Johnson, Joy and Dr. S. M., Mary Vondra and Martha Jo Church.
Pregnant – This Time It's Me. 1985. 24 pp. Centering Corporation,
Box 3367, Omaha, NE 68103-0367. $2.45.

Feelings – feeling scared, feeling angry, feeling sorry for oneself,
feeling guilty, and feeling alone – and dealing with these feelings are
stressed throughout this booklet.

Johnston, Patricia Irwin, Ed. *Perspectives on a Grafted Tree. 1983.* 144
pages. Perspectives Press, Hardcover. 144 pages. $12.95.

A beautiful collection of poems written by birthparents, adoptees,
adoptive parents, and extended family members. They express a
wide variety of both positive and negative feelings which are part of
the gains and losses, happiness and pain felt by all those touched by
adoption.

Lindsay, Jeanne Warren. *Do I Have a Daddy? A Story About a Single-
Parent Child.* Illustrated by DeeDee Upton Warr. 1982. 46 pp.
Color. Morning Glory Press, 6595 San Haroldo Way, Buena Park,
CA 90620. Hardcover, $7.95. Paper, $3.95.

This is a picture book/story in which a single mother explains to her
son that his daddy left soon after he was born. It contains a 12-page
section of suggestions for single parents, based on comments from
teenage mothers facing this question.

_____. *Open Adoption: A Caring Option.* 1987. 256 pp. Photos.
Morning Glory Press. Hardcover, $15.95; paper, $9.95.

A fascinating and sensitive account of the new world of adoption
where birthparents choose their child's adoptive parents and may
remain in contact with their child's new family. Written for birthparents, adoptive parents, and professionals.

_____. *Pregnant Too Soon: Adoption Is an Option. Revised* 1988.
124 pp. Morning Glory Press. Hardcover, $15.95; Paper, $9.95.
Teacher's Guide and Study Guide, 16 pp. ea., $2.00.

Young women who were, by their own admission, "pregnant too
soon," tell their stories. Most made the unpopular decision to release
for adoption. They share their reasons for doing so. Included with
the personal stories is information on agency and independent
adoption, fathers' rights, dealing with grief, and other aspects of
adoption. Especially written for young birthmothers.

_____. *Teenage Marriage: Coping with Reality. Revised 1988.* 208
pp. Photos. Morning Glory Press. Hardcover, $15.95. Paper, $9.95.
Teacher's guide, $5.95. Student study guide, $2.50.

Marriage book written especially for teenagers. Based on in-depth
interviews with married teens and on nationwide survey of teenagers' attitudes toward marriage. Extremely realistic.

_____. *Teens Look at Marriage: Rainbows, Roles and Reality.* 1985.
256 pp. Photos. Morning Glory Press. Hardcover, $15.95. Paper,
$9.95. Study Guide, $2.50.

An in-depth coverage of the research behind *Teenage Marriage:
Coping with Reality.* Attitudes of teenagers not yet married are
compared with those who are. Provides insight into world of teenage
couples. 34 bar graphs, 130 tables, 8 photos.

_____. *Teens Parenting: The Challenge of Babies and Toddlers.*
1981. 308 pp. Illustrated by Pam Patterson Morford. Morning Glory
Press. Hardcover, $14.95; paper, $9.95. TG, $5.95. SG, $2.50.

Basic how-to-parent book based on interviews with 61 teenage
mothers. Their comments are incorporated throughout the book.
Sixth grade reading level.

McGuire, Paula. *It Won't Happen to Me: Teenagers Talk About Pregnancy*. 1983. Delacourte, 234 pp. $14.95. Dell, 1986, $7.95.

Fifteen teenagers talk about their unplanned pregnancies, the decisions they made, and the changes in their lives.

Monserrat, Catherine, and Jeanne Lindsay. *Adoption Awareness: A Guide for Teachers, Nurses, Counselors and Caring Others*. 1989. Morning Glory Press, Inc. Hardcover, $17.95. Paper, $12.95.

Wonderful book for teachers, counselors, social workers, nurses, and others working with pregnant teenagers and/or older women facing untimely pregnancy. Offers an in-depth look at current adoption issues including agency, independent, and open adoption. Emphasis is on the needs of the birthparents.

Mueller, Candace P. *The Adoption Option: A Guidebook for Pregnancy Counselors*. 1986. 72 pages. Project SHARE, P.O. Box 2309, Rockville, MD 20852.

This guidebook was developed and written under the auspices of the Office of Population Affairs of the Department of Health and Human Services. It provides a general explanation of the adoption process and highlights important points that counselors should be aware of in counseling young women about adoption.

Myers, Walter Dean. *Sweet Illusions*. 1986. Available from Morning Glory Press. Paper, $3.95. Cloth, $9.95.

Absorbing fictional accounts of the lives of very young mothers and fathers. Eleven young people tell their stories, the whole threaded together by their involvement in the Piedmont Counseling Center. One story concerns a young woman who placed her child for adoption, considered getting him back two months later, then decided to leave him with his adoptive parents.

O'Brien, Bev. *Mom, I'm Pregnant*. 1982. Tyndale. 125 pp. $4.95.

Written by the mother of a pregnant teenager, this book has a strong religious slant. Emphasis is on the adoption decision.

Pierson, Anne. *Mending Hearts, Mending Lives*. 1987. Loving and Caring, Inc., 100 Foxshire Drive, Lancaster, PA 17601. 156 pp. Paper, $4.95.

Book written for families providing shelter in their homes for single pregnant women. Offers excellent guidance and shows real respect and caring for the young women involved.

Pierson, Anne. "My Baby and Me: Basic Decision-Making." 1984. Loving and Caring, Inc. 34-page workbook. $3.00.

Packed with "thinking" questions concerning goals in life, plans for the baby, and other areas of concern for pregnant teenagers.

Richards, Arlene Kramer, and Irene Willis. *What to Do If You or Someone You Know Is Under 18 and Pregnant.* 1983. 254 pp. Lothrop, $10.88. Paper, $7.00.

A very readable discussion of possible alternatives for pregnant teenagers.

Roggow, Linda, and Carolyn Owens. *A Handbook for Pregnant Teenagers.* Zondervan, Paper, $5.95.

Appropriate for young women whose religious convictions make abortion an impossible choice. Alternatives of marriage, adoption, and raising the baby alone are presented.

Rillera, Mary Jo, and Sharon Kaplan. *Cooperative Adoption: A Handbook.* 1984: Triadoption Publications, P.O. Box 638, Westminster, CA 92684. 158 pages. Paper. $14.95.

Offers excellent guidelines for birthparents and adoptive parents planning an open adoption. Authors do not recommend co-parenting except in the sense of both sets of parents being actively involved with the child. The adoptive parents are the legal and psychological day-to-day parents, but the birthparents may be as close to the adoptive family as desired by everyone involved. Suggested cooperative adoption documents are included.

Roles, Patricia. *Facing Teenage Pregnancy: A Handbook for the Pregnant Teen.* 1984. Eterna Press, P.O. Box 1344, Oak Brook, IL 60521. 123 pp. Paper, $5.95.

This is a personal guidebook with a non-directive and supportive approach. Included are several first-person accounts of early pregnancy, adoption, abortion, and parenthood.

Silber, Kathleen, and Phylis Speedlin. *Dear Birthmother: Thank You for Our Baby.* 1983. 193 pp. Corona Publishing Company, 1037 S. Alamo, San Antonio, TX 78210. Trade, $7.95.

An excellent book. Refutes such myths of adoption as the idea that birthparents don't care about their babies. Includes many beautiful letters from adoptive parents to birthparents and from birthparents to adoptive parents.

Sorosky, Arthur D., M.D., Annette Baran, and Reuben Pannor. *The Adoption Triangle: The Effects of the Sealed Record on Adoptees, Birthparents, and Adoptive Parents.* 1984. Doubleday. Paper, $9.95.

Probably the first book to promote more openness in adoption. The authors see adoption as a life-long process, and they suggest that we need to reform our attitudes and policies regarding adoption. They discuss the effects of reunion experiences between adoptees and their birthparents.

Witt, Reni L., and Jeannine Masterson Michael. *Mom, I'm Pregnant! A Personal Guide for Teenagers.* 1982. Stein & Day. 239 pp. $6.95.

Excellent book for young people facing decisions about unplanned pregnancy.

Zimmerman, Martha. *Should I Keep My Baby?* 112 pages. 1983. $3.95. Bethany House.

Offers help and direction for facing pregnancy outside of marriage. Argues against abortion, helps evaluate marriage, single motherhood, and adoption.

Audiotape: "Adoption Adventure: A Unique Collection of Songs About Adoption." 1986. Beth Lockhart, Adoptive Parents' Education Program, P.O. Box 32114, Phoenix, AZ 85064.

Wonderful collection of songs beautifully performed. My favorites are "Always Remember" and "I Will Tell Her You Love Her" (both for birthparents).

INDEX

ABOUT
THE AUTHOR

Jeanne Warren Lindsay, M.A., C.H.E., developed and for sixteen years coordinated the Teen Mother Program, an alternative offered to pregnant and parenting students in the ABC Unified School District, Cerritos, California. This program is a choice offered to pregnant and parenting students who do not wish to attend the comprehensive high school throughout pregnancy. Ms. Lindsay has counseled hundreds of pregnant teenagers. Many of these young women are rearing their children themselves while others have made and carried out adoption plans for their babies.

Ms. Lindsay has advanced degrees in home economics and anthropology. She is a volunteer consultant with the National Organization on Adolescent Pregnancy and Parenthood, and editor of the *NOAPP Network*. She frequently gives presentations on adoption, the culture of school-age parents, teenage marriage, educating pregnant and parenting teens, and other topics.

Ms. Lindsay has authored six other books dealing with adoption, adolescent pregnancy, parenthood, and teenage marriage. She is co-authoring with Catherine Monserrat the forthcoming *Adoption Awareness: A Guide for Teachers, Nurses, Counselors and Caring Others.*

Jeanne and Bob have been married 37 years, and they have five grown children.

OTHER BOOKS BY JEANNE WARREN LINDSAY

PREGNANT TOO SOON: Adoption Is an Option
Advocates choice. Young women who were, by their own admission, "pregnant too soon," tell their stories. Most made the unpopular decision to release for adoption. They share their reasons for doing so.

OPEN ADOPTION: A Caring Option
A fascinating and sensitive account of the new world of adoption. Read about birthparents choosing adoptive parents for their baby and adoptive parents maintaining contact with their baby's birthparents.

ADOPTION AWARENESS: A Guide for Teachers, Nurses, Counselors and Caring Others (with Catherine Monserrat)
Offers a philosophical framework and practical suggestions for presenting adoption as a choice. Guidelines for assisting birthparents in the classroom, in the counseling setting, and in the hospital.

TEENS PARENTING: The Challenge of Babies and Toddlers
Parenting book written especially for teenage parents. Classroom-tested, easy to read, realistic and practical. Lots of quotes from teen parents.

TEENAGE MARRIAGE: Coping with Reality
Gives teenagers a picture of the realities of marriage – a look at the difficulties they may encounter if they say "I do". . .or simply move in together . . .too soon.

TEENS LOOK AT MARRIAGE: Rainbows, Roles and Reality
Helps you understand the culture of teenage couples. Includes statistical information about teenagers' attitudes toward marriage and living together. Attitudes of teenagers not yet married are compared with those who are.

DO I HAVE A DADDY? A Story About a Single-Parent Child
Picture/story book especially for children with only one parent. Includes special ten-page section for single parent.

Books by Linda Barr and Catherine Monserrat:
TEENAGE PREGNANCY: A New Beginning
Prenatal health book written especially for pregnant teenagers. Covers not only the medical, but also the social and practical aspects of being a pregnant or parenting teen.

WORKING WITH CHILDBEARING ADOLESCENTS
Designed for use by professionals from various disciplines. Will help improve effectiveness in working with pregnant teenagers and teenage parents.

Please see other side for ordering information.

MORNING GLORY PRESS
6595 San Haroldo Way, Buena Park, CA 90620
714/828-1998

Please send me the following:

Quantity	Title	Price	Total

Parents, Pregnant Teens and the Adoption Option

____	Paper, ISBN 0-930934-28-8	8.95	_____
____	Cloth, ISBN 0-930934-29-6	13.95	_____

Adoption Awareness

____	Paper, ISBN 0-930934-32-6	$12.95	_____
____	Cloth, ISBN 0-930934-33-4	17.95	_____

Pregnant Too Soon: Adoption Is an Option

____	Paper, ISBN 0-930934-25-3	$9.95	_____
____	Cloth, ISBN 0-930934-26-1	15.95	_____

Open Adoption: A Caring Option

____	Paper, ISBN 0-930934-23-7	9.95	_____
____	Cloth, ISBN 0-930934-22-9	15.95	_____

Teenage Pregnancy: A New Beginning

____	Spiral	10.00	_____

Working with Childbearing Adolescents

____	Spiral	12.95	_____

Teens Parenting: The Challenge of Babies and Toddlers

____	Paper, ISBN 0-930934-06-7	9.95	_____
____	Cloth, ISBN 0-930934-07-5	14.95	_____

Teenage Marriage: Coping with Reality

____	Paper, ISBN 0-930934-30-x	9.95	_____
____	Cloth, ISBN 0-930934-31-8	15.95	_____

Teens Look at Marriage: Rainbows, Roles and Reality

____	Paper, ISBN 0-930934-15-6	9.95	_____
____	Cloth, ISBN 0-930934-16-4	15.95	_____

Do I Have a Daddy? A Story About a Single-Parent Child

____	Paper, ISBN 0-930934-17-2	3.95	_____
____	Cloth, ISBN 0-930934-10-5	7.95	_____

TOTAL _____

Please add postage: 1-4 books, $2.00; 5+, .50 per book _____
California residents - add 6% sales tax _____

TOTAL ENCLOSED _____

Ask about quantity discounts, Teacher's Guides, Study Guides.

Prepayment requested. School/library purchase orders accepted.
If not satisfied, return in 15 days for refund.

NAME _____

ADDRESS_____

_____